UNDERCOVER

THE UNTOLD STORY OF ALQAEDA
THE FBI AND CIA IN AMERICA

EMAD SALEM

FEBRUARY 26, 1993, 12:17:37 P.M.

A bomb explodes in the B-2 level at
the Twin Towers of the World Trade
Center.

A half billion dollars of damage is
nothing compared to the over 1,000
injuries...

and the 7 deaths:

John DiGiovanni

Bob Kirkpatrick

Steven Knapp

Bill Macko

Willie Mercado

Monica Smith and Baby Boy Smith

To the innocent souls of
these seven victims of a
senseless, needless and
cowardly act of terror,
I dedicate this book

My name is Emad. I was born in a Box.
I escaped from the Box, and now Emad is gone.

PREFACE

Other books and accounts have been written of the first World Trade Center Bombing in February 1993 and of the subsequent Day of Terror Bust that prevented the "Landmark Bombings," also in New York.

They have been written by some players in the saga and by bystanders recounting after the fact. Journalists have tried to make a name for themselves, and succeeded. The Federal Prosecutor, Andrew McCarthy, who I admire immensely, has written his account from his perspective. But none of them were inside the cell. None of them heard the voices and the plans, felt the intensity and the anxiety, or put their lives on the line day after day.

I lived, ate and slept with the terrorists in the basement of the mosques and homes and I was able to dissect and digest their way of thinking and their personalities.

I did.

None of them lives in hiding, unable to use his real name or travel freely.

I do.

I am in a unique position to help the American people understand what is wrong about our war on terrorism and to show how to start winning that war and how these evildoers think.

My experience also obligates me to point out the human shortcomings that go uncensored and uncorrected in the Federal law enforcement organizations. I explain some of the ways personal feelings and personality conflicts caused or nearly caused disasters. I call for self-inspection and self-correction, so those who put their lives on the line are safer and more effective on behalf of the American people.

PART I

CHAPTER ONE
Being Emad

Cairo, Egypt

On February 22, 1950, I arrived into the Salem family. Ali, my father, was a stern disciplinarian, and my dear mother, Bothaina Noman, made me feel safe. Aladin was only one year old when I was born. Four years later, Fatma joined us, completing our Salem family.

As I grew older, roles changed. My father became my mentor, my mother was my confidant, and Aladin, for all his artistic temperament, was my athletic coach when I began wrestling in preparatory schools (junior high school). In turn, I became Fatma's protector and guide in life.

I had a happy childhood in a good family - a solid, educated, and westernized family. No camels; no crocodiles; nothing stereotypically Egyptian, outwardly. I even attended an American school. This fact probably, in the end, saved many American lives.

The Salem's Family

That elementary school had a great impact on my life. Miss Matilda and Miss Inga – I still remember their names! – Taught us all day long, with the American flag hanging above our chalkboard. Then, every day - lunchtime! I still love the sharp cheddar cheese I first tasted there and the chocolate powder we mixed in our milk.

*Emad S. in the upper right hand corner
in the American School in Cairo*

School was a very pleasant introduction to the USA. I loved the America that sent me tasty food and nice teachers. America and the American flag became visions in my subconscious mind.

But America and the American flag and American food were, in reality, far outside the box into which I was born.

My father taught in the military academy, so when I was old enough,

Cadet Emad Salem

he directed me there. After high school, I spent four years in college earning a degree in electronics. The day I graduated as a Lt. Engineer, I was 24 years old.

Another Family

I never had a girlfriend. Islam instructs you to honor a woman by marrying her and giving her your name before you are intimate with her. I chose to respect the tenets of Islam.

At age 24, I had graduated from military college and felt ready for a wife. My father was not inclined to arrange a marriage for me, so I set out to deliberately and logically find a wife for myself.

Four girls seemed to be possibilities. One was my sister's friend, Wafeh. Salwa was my cousin on my mother's side, and Naima and the fourth girl were my first cousins on my father's side. In America, marriage with first cousins is frowned upon; but in Egypt, marriage within the family is accepted and even preferred. Very normal.

With the four names on a piece of paper, I created divisions: "Social," "Educational," and so on. Under each category, I ranked each young lady. Simple as that. Naima ranked the highest.

When I told my father I wanted to get married and thought Naima would be a good match, he agreed. "Oh, Naima! That's great. She's a great kid." I invited him to go with me to propose. "No, you go." It was one of his ways of teaching me independence.

First, I approached Naima's mother, who accepted the idea very well. Then Naima's father gave his consent. We became engaged. After approval from the Health department (to test for genetic abnormalities, because we were closely related), I paid the *mahr*, or dowry. Her deputy – in this case, her father – and I signed a contract.

Our wedding was held at her house in Cairo, blessed by an Imam. After the ceremony, we went into the heart of Cairo, to a night club on the River Nile, for dinner and a night of dancing. That was the extent of our honeymoon.

We moved into an apartment in Cairo and began our life together. She was about eighteen and just finishing high school. I wanted my wife to be educated. Naima had good grades, so she applied and was admitted to law school.

For four years, I was a military officer by day, and by night I went to the market, cooked dinner and cleaned up, and did laundry in the bathtub. I wanted her to do nothing but study. We put off having children so she would be free to concentrate her time and effort on her studies. In her fourth year, we stopped using contraceptives, and six months later she became pregnant with Noha, our daughter.

After Naima's graduation, my connections and contacts paid off. Through my network of friends, I got her a very safe, secure position as an attorney in the state of Cairo.

Four years after Noha, our son, Sherif (*honored*; *honest*), was born.

My First Family

Over the years, Naima and I had our problems. In another era, we might have stayed together, both unhappy. But this was modern Egypt. We finally separated, the children staying with her.

Taking Care of Business

During the day, I was a military officer. Now free in the evenings, I started a private business, the first of many. One of my businesses was Computer Training Institute, "CTI." Zohar Kady, a Lebanese man, was my partner. He did the educational side, and I did the public relations side. At that time, in the mid- to late-seventies, computers were entering a new era. Punch cards were gone. People were beginning to use MS-DOS, and there was a need for training. We had students from every bank in Cairo.

Unfortunately, when we added another partner, he and Zohar had a falling-out. He reported Zohar for being a non-citizen involved in business. The result was Zohar's deportation from Egypt. I was able to protect his business interests until I could help his wife get back to Lebanon where he was. Then I delivered his money to him, as well, so he didn't lose everything.

The next business I started was with Yousri Hegazi, a wealthy Egyptian. We created Noras ("seagull") Advertising for media production.

One of our productions was a play called *Appointment with the Ambassador*. Yousri got a producer named Faiza to work on it. It's been shown on television; I made good money from that project.

Faiza and I immediately fell for each other. I was already separated at that time from Naima, though we were not yet divorced. Islam allows a man to have up to four wives at a time. So I married Faiza.

I moved in with her. She had a palace! For the first time in my life, I saw a round bed. When I sat on it, it rotated! Lying on it, you looked up into navy blue mirrors. Life with Faiza was a two-year honeymoon. She made me think I was a gorgeous, handsome guy. She made me think so many wonderful things…

One day I opened a closet, and there was a big package of hashish. "What's this?"

She said, casually, "Oh it's hash. Don't worry about it."

"I DO worry about it! I'm an officer in the military! Are you crazy?" No reply. "You've got to stop this right away. Otherwise…" I waited.

She answered me. "Ok. Bye."

It isn't hard to get a divorce in Egypt.

CHAPTER TWO
THINK Outside the Box

"*Think.*" This was the sign I always kept on my desk. I needed this reminder. Thinking was not strongly encouraged in the culture where I worked and lived.

Emad Salem in office

With full respect to where I was born, it is a fact that Egypt is a Third World country. Education is not greatly emphasized in the culture as a whole. Society has a very limited vision.

You put blinders on a horse to keep him from being distracted. He can't see what's going on in the world around him, so it doesn't interest him. The only thing that exists for him is what is put in front of him. His master imposes that narrow view upon him.

Growing up in Egypt is like having on mental blinders. You're only exposed to certain limited viewpoints. Whatever is thrown at you, you begin to absorb. This is the Middle Eastern "box" into which I was born.

Cracks in my box developed as I learned the value of thinking. It has always been important to me to use my brain. I try to be around people who think. But thinkers do not long remain in boxes imposed upon them through no choice of their own. Thinkers resist boxes.

One major philosophy planted in my mind from an early age is that Jews are some sort of vicious beasts. The pictures in the Egyptian newspapers show an Egyptian soldier with his big boot heel stepping on a little tiny midget with big eyes, a big nose, big ears, and sometimes with horns and tails. That's how the Jews were portrayed. So many Egyptians that I've met have this idea that Jews are devils, so they are obviously anti-Jewish.

But one day, I was exposed to some Jewish prisoners from the 1973 war. I saw them myself. They had eyes! My God, they were sweating, trembling. They were afraid. They weren't demons at all. Among them was a female sergeant.

1973 Jewish War Prisoners

For some reason, I found myself actually surprised that the Jews were human beings. I was a military officer, but suddenly, there was a great big crack in my box - the first of many to come.

The Fixer

In every deserted place, you have a ghost. ~ Ancient Proverb
I had "ghosts."

I worked my way up through the military and became a Lt. Colonel. God gave me the ability to make contacts and connections everywhere I went. If my friends, or the friends of my friends, needed anything, someone would say, "Call Emad. He will get it done." Emad, the Fixer.

In the police department, I had connections. In the State Department I had connections. In the media, too. I even had contacts in the department that collected the garbage!

A friend of Yousri was considering getting an apartment. She gave the landlord a down payment of thirty thousand Egyptian pounds. She trusted him; there was no receipt, nothing. But later, she changed her mind about the place and wanted her money back. The landlord said she had to sleep with him to get it back.

One day she was crying about this to Yousri. She needed that money back, but she wasn't going to sleep with the guy. Yousri said, "I know how to get your money. I'm going to call Emad Salem." He picked up the phone and told me her story.

I said, "Give me her name."

I sat with her and got the details. She gave me the address of the guy. Then four plainclothes soldiers and I got in my jeep. We barged into this guy's cocoon. He was smoking hashish.

I confronted him. "One of two things is going to happen here tonight. Either I take you, and you vanish for the rest of your life, or you're going to get the thirty thousand pounds you took from Inas and return it to me so I can give it back to her."

"I don't have it," he answered.

"Ok." I turned calmly to the soldiers. "Put the black hood on his head. I'm taking him."

"OK! OK! I'll get it!" He got the idea. He took a picture off the wall, opened the safe behind it, and gave me thirty thousand pounds in cash, right there. I wrapped it in newspaper and gave it back to Inas that night.

She and I have been good friends ever since.

I'm not saying I'm a good guy for barging into somebody's cocoon. But I did what I had to do to save this woman's money.

It wasn't for any payment I helped others when I could. It gave me pleasure to see justice done.

Brutality crushed my box

Shattered!

I have some good friends, as I mentioned, in the Federal Division. I used to go sit with them when they worked very late at night. One night, about 3:00 a.m., one of them said to me, "Do you want to go to the basement with me? They need me down there."

"Sure."

"Are you really sure? Do you have a strong heart?"

"Of course!" Usually they have suspects down there, under arrest. I was a Major in the Egyptian military, and I thought I had seen everything already. So I went with him. But when the metal door in that freezing basement squeaked open…

"Torture" doesn't even begin to describe it.

Under a bright light hung a stark naked Egyptian, strung up by his ankles, arms dangling toward the floor. It was so cold, and he had nothing on, but that was the least of his problems.

A *khaboor* is a cone shaped piece of wood. It gets answers from people.

The pointed tip of the khaboor is slipped into the anal opening of the upside-down detainee. The first question is asked. And when the answer is not "correct," – and it rarely is - BANG! A wooden hammer slams the khaboor in a couple inches. The next question is asked, and if they don't hear what they want to hear, BANG!

I did not ever think a human being could be dealt with in this manner. This naked Egyptian, hanging upside down, being tortured in this way, blew me away. I couldn't let on how I was affected, but my thinking brain began to consider the future. I asked myself, "Tonight, I am here as a major. But, someday, could this happen to me or one of my children?"

With that thought, my Box was completely and utterly shattered. At that moment, I knew I could not continue to live in that environment.

I began to put into motion my retirement.

I had served eighteen years with the Egyptian military. Because some of those were during war, I was credited with twenty-four years of service. This gave me a pension and started me on the dream that had been in the back of my mind and in the depths of my heart since I was seven years old. My dream of America and the American flag had stuck with me for thirty-seven long years.

Emad S. at the time of retirement

By the time I was preparing to live in America, Naima and I had been separated for some time. She did not want to make the move to America with me, and so she asked me for a divorce, which I gave her. I wanted her to be happy. When she fell in love with her boss, I hosted their marriage in my apartment. The children stayed with Naima, and I gave my pension for their expenses. Today Naima is the director of the legal department in the State of Cairo, and her husband is legal director in another section.

CHAPTER THREE
The American Dream

In 1987, I lived my dream. I came to America! Sharp cheddar cheese, chocolate milk, and the American flag!

Welcome to My America

When I was born in Egypt, it was not by my choice. America is my choice. And usually when we choose something, it is ten thousand times more valuable than something that is imposed on us.

The day I became an American citizen was like I had gone to heaven. People might laugh at me, but that was how I felt. America is what I cherish. I have my children in America. My wife is in America. And this is where I have bought my grave. This is my home.

I will do whatever it takes to keep my America safe and sound.

And make no mistake about it. I will not allow ANYONE to try to harm my America. You will have to deal with me.

New York, New York!

In New York, I got a job with the Chatwel Inn. The Manhattan hotel is owned by an Indian man, who also owns several other hotels, and he put me in charge of engineering, repairs and security in several of his hotels. I was doing ok.

Emad S. at Woodward Hotel

I was single at the time, living in an apartment in the hotel, on the Upper West Side, 55th and Broadway. One of my neighbors would come over to watch TV, late at night. At times, she came in an evening gown. But I never touched Miriam. Sometimes she would come at 2:00 or 3:00 a.m. I never made a move on her.

One day she had the guts to ask, "Are you gay?"

"Nooo…Why would you ask me that?"

"Why aren't you going out? You only go to the gym, and you sit home all the time. And you aren't attracted to me."

"How do you know? I climb the walls after you leave!"

"So what's wrong?"

I answered, "Nothing. I just choose to abide by my religion. I cannot touch any woman unless I am married to her."

That was, I guess, very appealing to Miriam's ear. "Oh my God, I respect you for that! I think you would be very suitable for my friend Karin."

Karin, a jewelry designer from Germany, was working for a company on 47th St., and she always had lunch with her co-worker, Miriam. Miriam gave me Karin's number, and I called her up and asked her out.

Now Miriam had already prepared Karin for my call. "Well, if anything, you won't have a boring evening. He's really charming and he can talk."

Karin was thinking, "Oh well, what can I lose?" When I called her she responded in a very American way. "Let me look at my schedule…Let's see, I have an opening on Wednesday…"

"What?!" I said. "I'm not waiting on anybody!" And hung up.

Miriam, fortunately, convinced me to try again. I took her for Italian food, and over *nerodi seppia* (spaghetti in octopus ink) interrogated her! Karin doesn't hide anything. She was open and honest with me. We continued to see each other, but I never slept with her.

It was whirlwind courtship, really. Maybe three months. I cooked for her. (I cooked better than she did; perhaps she married me for the *Missakaa*.) We talked and got to know each other. I told her I wasn't coming into the relationship alone; I had two children in Egypt. That didn't bother her. In fact, she welcomed the idea, as she didn't have any kids of her own. Her reaction to having my kids around moved me to propose. And one day, I did; I asked her to marry me.

In Germany, getting married isn't all that important, even if you have children together. Karin had already tried marriage twice and really preferred her free, uncomplicated life in her beautiful apartment in The Bretton-Hall on Broadway. Her career was everything to her. She really wasn't ready to give it all up. "Are you crazy? We don't know each other yet!" She cried.

But I chose to stick to the backbone of my religion. I gave an ultimatum. "Midnight tonight. Otherwise, goodbye."

We found two Arabic speaking witnesses. I had a written contract made, and I paid her a symbolic dowry. We had rings, because she was a jeweler. Done by midnight. Married!

We had a wonderful honeymoon. Our chemistry was right. That was 1991. Other than a brief separation in 2009, when we foolishly thought we could live without each other, we have been together ever since.

Shortly after we were married, I found out my pension was not being used to take care of my children as I intended. Naima's new husband was abusing the use of my pension money for himself. So I applied for custody of the kids and got it. On Christmas Eve, 1991, seven- year-old Sherif and eleven-year-old Noha joined us in America. Karin was glad to have them. Our family was complete and together.

My Second Family

CHAPTER FOUR
My America

A Chance to Help

We Middle Easterners always assume the Americans are extremely sophisticated. Especially the FBI. We thought every FBI agent had the equivalent of a small satellite in his pocket and could see and hear everything, everywhere! Growing up watching movies from America, I always saw the FBI portrayed as invincible. That is the world perception of the FBI: invincible. Right? They are James Bond, Double O's, and Supermen.

This was still my thinking the day Nancy Floyd walked into my office at the Woodward hotel in early 1991.

Special Agent Nancy Floyd

"I'm an FBI agent." And she showed me her badge. I was very happy to be in the presence of an FBI agent, even though she didn't look much like James Bond. Then she blew me away.

"I need your help."

My God! MY help!?

"Do you know there are some Russians staying in your hotel?" Nancy was a Special Agent in the FBI's Russian office in New York City.

"Yes. I'm aware of that. Rooms number x and y."

"I need to know what is in their garbage cans and their phone records."

"Ok, I have a master key. Let's go to their rooms." I wanted to help America in any possible way.

"Oh no, I can't go to their room, because I don't have a search warrant."

I was shocked! "What? What do you mean? You're the FBI!"

She smiled. "I can't. All I want is their garbage and phone records"

So I said, "Just give me 'til tomorrow. Let's have some lunch in TGI Fridays, and I'll see what I can do."

I didn't, and still don't, know if they were KGB or the Russian mafia. To be quite honest I couldn't resist the temptation of going an extra mile on my own and using my master key to see what else I can gather besides what agent Nancy asked for. Either way, bad for my job – and my neck! - If they found me in their room. All I knew, in 1991, was that these were Russians, and this was my America. I'm not going to let anyone mess with my America. I gathered all that was in the trashcans and I got a copy of their phone records.

I went up to the Russians' rooms. I opened briefcases and collected documents. So as not to leave anything out of place, I made copies for Nancy Floyd even though she didn't ask for it, I thought I could provide her with more information so I can be more helpful. I thought if I will be able to collect their fingerprints that might be helpful as well. There were cigarettes in the room, so I noted their brand. I bought some new packs. I took the cellophane, with their fingerprints, off their cigarette packs and replaced it with the cellophane from the new packs that I handled with gloves. I delivered everything to Nancy Floyd, who was surprised and impressed with what I was able to put in her hands. We kept this up for about six months.

There came a time when Nancy showed me someone's picture and asked me if I can Identify him since the CIA was interested in verifying his identity. Luckily I knew that individual so I verified him and provided her with his name and information. I think that was helpful for the CIA purpose of verification and I also think that the information I provided her with was corroborated.

Another Project

At one point Nancy asked, "Would you mind helping INS?"

"Who? I never met him."

She laughed. "No, the INS is the Immigration and Naturalization Service."

I said, "Oh! OK. As long as it's in America, I'm willing to do it."

She introduced me to Kyle Hutchinson, an INS detective. He said they needed information on the illegal workers at the hotels where I had worked. There were about 130 employees at the three hotels. Kyle would come every morning at 5:00 am. I sat in his car with him as I took a picture of each person walking into work. To prove who was who and what was what, I got Kyle copies of employee names and their time sheets.

I gave Kyle the backdoor keys and told him about the Indian manager's signal, "Code Red." Singh, the manager, had told the illegal workers that if immigration walked through the front door, he would radio them the "Code Red" signal and they should all go out the back door.

As I was gathering information on terrorists and working with the FBI agents, they would appear from time to time at my office in the hotel. During this operation, my boss, Mr. Singh, noticed these agents coming and going and confronted me about them. When they showed him their badges, he immediately fired me. On the spot. He made a wild accusation that I was probably working with INS as well. Little did he know.

We had enough information from inside the hotel, fortunately, for INS to make their sting and complete that operation.

When the INS agents came in the lobby, they grabbed the radios so the code couldn't be sent out. By the time someone got up to Singh's office to send out the code, INS had their trucks outside the back door, and the employees walked out the back door into the INS trucks.

The agent prepared it right and got all his warrants. It was a good case, a very good case, for the Feds.

Fired

In the fall of 1991, while I was still gathering information for INS, Nancy asked if I would go a little further. "I'd like to introduce you to the terrorist squad. Will you assist them?"

"As long as they are Americans, I'd be glad to."

Nancy introduced me to John Anticev, another FBI agent, and Louie Napoli, an NYPD detective working in the Joint Terrorism Task Force (JTTF).

We talked about the killing of a Jewish rabbi in Manhattan sometime the year before. El Sayyid Nosair was accused of shooting Rabbi Kahane at the Eastside Marriot on Nov. 5, 1990. His trial was happening at a courthouse in Manhattan, and I was asked to hang around, try to get close to Nosair's followers, and report what was being said among them.

I replied, "Sure, I'm off tomorrow. I'll go down and see what I can find out." And that was the beginning of something much bigger than I could have imagined.

Up to this time, I had been working without any payments from the Feds, about nine months. Now, however, I had lost my job from helping them. I had a new wife and had recently brought my kids to the States from Egypt. I had to be able to support my family; I began to job hunt, obviously.

Nancy, however, had another idea. She asked for my pay stubs from my hotel job. I was earning about $500 a week. She was able to get approval from Carson Dunbar, the Assistant Special Agent in Charge (ASAC) in the FBI, for me to receive the same pay from the FBI if I would continue to work for them. I agreed. This was the first time I was paid for any of my work with the FBI, and getting paid was not my idea. It was offered to me as compensation, only to replace my hotel salary.

CHAPTER FIVE
What You Don't Know CAN Hurt You

"What is the biggest terror organization that threatens the United States, and who was its leader?" I would bet you answered, "Al Qaeda and Osama bin Laden." Sorry. Wrong.

Does that scare you? Is it frightening to think there is an organization bigger than Al Qaeda or a leader more threatening than bin Laden was? Perhaps you should be frightened, but perhaps not.

Who IS the enemy, anyway?

Know your enemy.

Americans are not really aware of who their enemy is.

This is a problem not just for Americans taking off their shoes in airports and having their backpacks searched at sporting events. The CIA, FBI and all their relatives continue very much disorganized in their knowledge of the identities, motives, thought patterns and means of their enemies.

I was amazed at how little American agents, tasked with making and handling contacts, knew about the Middle Eastern culture and mind-set. Usually inadvertently, I like to believe; those who needed my help often offended me. Also inadvertently, my actions and concerns were misinterpreted by my contacts on more than one occasion. One of those misunderstandings resulted in six lost lives. But I will get to that.

I do not write this to criticize my fellow Americans whose job it is to protect us from terrorism. Actually, I have conducted presenations for the FBI to help rectify this lack of cross-cultural understanding. Agent Dan Coleman knew of my work and invited me to give presentations in the FBI Academy in Quantico, Virginia to help resolve some of these issues and save our agents some embarrassing or even dangerous situations.

Special Agent Dan Coleman (The Professor)

Hopefully, such unfortunate incidents are now happening less often, and the US is better able to receive help from Middle Easterners who want only to live in peace with their non-Muslim neighbors on earth.

When I am giving my presentations, I start with a gesture, waving my hand. The agents reply, "Hello." I was not saying "hello." That gesture means "come here." If you use the usual American gesture for "come here," the hand lifted, palm toward yourself, wiggling your index finger, a Middle Easterner will take great offense. You have just sneered at him and called him an S.O.B.

Here in the U.S., if I am working with you, and you introduce me to your wife, I may tell you – or her- that she is very beautiful. You will be pleased and take that as a compliment. However, if an agent working the Middle East says this to one of his contacts there, he is now in very deep trouble, for he will be considered flirting with his colleague's wife. This is worse than flirting in the U.S., because Middle Eastern men are quite possessive and jealous of their women. Perhaps protective is a better term. We have a saying, "For my wife, I lose my life." While an American man also might lay his life on the line for his wife or daughter, the life goes on the line much more quickly in the Middle Eastern culture, and U.S. agents do well to stay back from that line. You do not want to piss off your contact; you REALLY don't want to die for it.

You can get badly hurt over something you did not even know you did not know!

What You Didn't Know You Didn't Know

This is where I can be of help in my presentations. There exist three kinds of knowledge:

1. The things you know. You know you know them. Your address. Your name. How to balance a checkbook. How to drive your car. Who is the president? Stuff like that.

2. The things you don't know, and you know you don't know them. You are aware that you don't know how to build a rocket ship, but you know that information does exist.

3. There are things you don't know, and you don't know that you don't know them.

My job, and that of other operatives undercover, is to find out what the Feds don't know that they don't know. You can't find the answers if you do not know the questions. My job was to start finding the important questions. Sometimes, I found answers, and we had to backtrack to discover what unknown questions they answered.

In helping you understand what was happening when I came into the picture in New York, I must tell you a little about Islamic terrorists and where they come from. It's what you don't know that you don't know.

CHAPTER SIX
Who's an Infidel?

The Prophet Mohammad (PBUH) married a Jewish woman and a Christian woman. Allah had him do this to show that we should be colorblind and tolerant. We should not allow our religious differences to separate us.

A verse in the Quran defines an infidel. The interpretation of it is this. "You who are infidels: I don't worship who you worship, and you don't worship who I worship. And I will not worship who you worship, and you will not worship who I worship. You've got your beliefs; I've got mine." (Holy Quran, Verse 109) The verse is finished. I don't see where God said, "I'm going to go kill you because you are an infidel."

This verse calls the infidel (*kaffiroon*). This is someone who does not believe in God and rejects the Scriptures. Christians and Jews believe in God. They accept the Bible and the Torah, and the Quran all three scriptures. Nobody can call them infidels.

I am a Muslim who is living in America by choice, and I will never, ever allow anyone to harm my America. I want the American people to know that it's ok to be a Christian and a believer. If I help you in a time of need, I will be rewarded on the Day of Judgment if I help you, because you are a believer. That's what the Quran says. When I look at you, I see the human race. I love you as a human being regardless of your beliefs.

In the lines of every man's palm are the Arabic numbers one and eight. This is in each hand, so when the numbers are added, you have ninety-nine. This is a God-given signature, because we say God has ninety-nine names. This signature unifies us as God's creation.

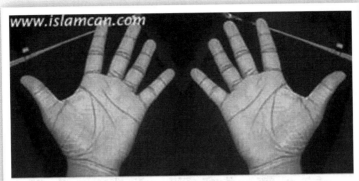

Look at your hands and identify the outlined marks.

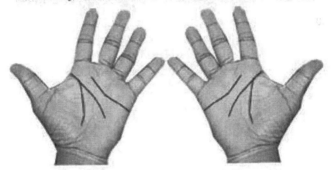

In Arabic, 8 is written as $\wedge$ and 1 is written as $|$. Thus, on your left hand, the marks appear as $\wedge|$ which can be written as 81 in English. On the right hand, the marks appear as $|\wedge$, which can be written as 18. Here is the interesting part, if you were to add 81 and 18, it becomes 99, which is the number of Allah's beautiful names that appear in the Quran. Also, if you subtract 18 from 81, it becomes 63. At the age of 63, Prophet Muhammad (peace be upon him) passed away and the religion of Islam was completed! Amazing, isn't it? It is as if the Kalimah is written on your hands. There is no god but Allah and Muhammad is the messenger of Allah.

Look at your fingers – ten of them. God gave Ten Commandments. You believe this whether you are Muslim, Jewish or Christian. So if you pray in a Mosque, a synagogue, or a church, you are still carrying those same Ten Commandments and the signature of God. What are we fighting about? You have all that you need to follow the Ten Commandments. You have the signature of God in your hands, so don't sin with them.

Radical Islamists don't like to talk about this in public, because they don't want to help a Christian or a Jewish person. Most of the radical Middle Easterners have this idea embedded in their minds that these people are the enemies, that they are the infidels.

The Quran contains a verse that identifies the believer. Five pillars. He who believes in:

1. God

2. God's angels

3. God's prophets – Abraham, Isaac, Jacob, Jesus, and Mohamed (PBUH).

4. The Holy Scriptures- the Torah, the Bible, and the Quran.

5. The Day of Judgment.

Believing in these five things, you are a believer, according to the Quran.

No one has the power to categorize you as an infidel. This is something between you and God, because it is a matter of faith. Only God can tell what your heart believes. I certainly cannot say you are an infidel, and neither can any sheik.

However, there are men with agendas. These men have stretched, twisted, and changed the message of Islam, looking for power or money or both.

To serve their agenda, they mislead people who are not educated in religious matters. These people might be engineers or doctors, but they are not educated enough to dig into the meaning of Islam.

These so called religious leaders teach that any non-Muslim is an infidel. This is not true. They have twisted the words of God and the Prophet (PBUH) to say something else, something that will help them achieve what they want. I heard Sheik Omar say in one of his lectures, "I am a terrorist. God asked me to be a terrorist, and I am proud to be one." He based this on his interpretation of a verse in the Quran where God says, "When I prepare my horse and my strength and my army, my enemy will fear me." This word "fear" is sometimes translated "terror." But there is no aggression here. It did say "prepare steeds of war," but this is just to be ready, so you will be feared and respected by God's enemy and your enemy. It does not tell you to actively attack anybody or kill them. This would be aggression, and that is forbidden in the Quran. It is true, you can fight infidels, but jihad, which means "duty" or "task," does not have to be interpreted in a military way. In context of Islam, it should not be aggressive.

Sheik Omar Abdel Rahman

You may read this and think, "Ok, these are two different persons' interpretations of the Quran. It just depends on how you want to read it. No, this is not so. I looked up the verses verbatim for myself.

I studied them. I have no reason to manipulate the interpretation. I am a benign person, not against Christians or Jews. I am a Muslim who is living in America by choice. I have no agenda. I just read the Quran to find out what God wants to say to me.

Perhaps you wonder if I am reading a different version of the Quran. There are no different versions of the Quran. Not a Sunni version and a Shiite version. Absolutely not. The Quran has not changed in thousands of years and will not change. According to the Quran, God's angel, Gabriel, gave all the words to Prophet Mohamed (PBUH). Prophet Mohamed (PBUH) could not read or write. He recited, and his friends wrote it down. He was like a radio from God. Therefore, none of it can be changed.

But recently, this very small group of radical people has gotten the upper hand. They manipulate the facts and misinterpreted God's words to label someone an infidel so they can create permission to kill him. They make jihad a military term and tell young people they have a duty to kill infidels.

The Feds need to understand and use this information about radical Islamic leaders and where they get their power. They must understand these people are not willing to have peace talks or make deals that they will never honor. American authorities must get inside the heads of their enemies and act accordingly to protect the American way of life that is valued by people all around the world.

The First Group of the Muslim Brotherhood

CHAPTER SEVEN
The Muslim Brotherhood

What is the biggest terror organization that threatens the United States, and who was its leader?

In 1928, an Arabic language teacher, Mr. Hassan El Banna and six manual laborers agreed to establish The Group of Muslim Brotherhood to preserve and spread Islamic law. They elected Mr. Banna, aged 22, to be their Leader.

For ten years, the group worked to establish itself. But in 1938, El Banna announced to his followers the beginning of the jihad period. He ordered the establishment of a military wing, called "The Secret Organization".

The group's goal was to drive out British occupation from Egypt. In 1946, Gamal Abdel Nasser and Anwar El Sadat were recruited to the cause, bringing with him several of his colleagues. They all swore allegiance to El Banna.

Hassan El Banna

In November of 1947, The United Nations decision dividing Palestine caused the Secret Organization to begin warring against the westerners and the Jewish Community. The Secret Organization continued violent attacks against government officials and Jewish businesses. On December 8, 1948, the Egyptian Government announced Marshal Law, dismantled the Muslim Brotherhood, seized all of their assets and imprisoned many of the members.

In the early fifties, Syed Qutb returned from a work assignment in San Francisco, California, U.S.A.

Syed Qutb

He had gone there with high hopes of meshing Islam with the other cultures of the world. But what he saw in San Francisco quickly disillusioned him: women kissing men on the street corners. Even American manicured lawns made him sick, a sign of western decadence. By the time he returned to Egypt after three years in the U.S., his disappointment had turned to hatred.

Back home he communicated with a fellow-Egyptian, Hassan El Banna, joined the Muslim Brotherhood, and became an active leader. Qutb thought the Muslim Brotherhood would go through three phases: establishing itself, struggling/fighting to gain power, and then a victory period in which Islam would rule above or in place of secular governments across Europe through Asia. Believing the establishment period was past and the struggle had begun, Qutb adopted a philosophy of violence for his organization.

The symbol of the Muslim Brotherhood depicts two swords below the Quran, with the motto, "Prepare to Fight the Infidel." The tragedy was, whoever they didn't like was an "infidel." They have made *jihad* mean "Holy War."

The Muslim Brotherhood logo

In 1952, Gamal Abdel Nasser replaced the last king of Egypt, King Farouk, and became the first Egyptian President. Nasser's emphasis was a secular government for Egypt, but he released the Muslim Brotherhood members out into Egyptian society. In return, they plotted an assassination (that never took place).

Let this attempt on their own member remind us that the Muslim Brotherhood's goal of rule by Islamic law supersedes all other loyalties, including the lives of its own members who do not cooperate. Why would this organization ever negotiate with America, the country it hates more than any other? There could never exist a treaty between the Muslim Brotherhood and a free democratic nation that would really be honored.

Waxing and waning in strength throughout the past decades, in turn outlawed and then supported in many Middle Eastern countries, the Muslim Brotherhood and its offshoots and arms and sub-groups continue to exert power around the world. Recently, with the Arab Spring movement, the Muslim Brotherhood seemed to gain a considerable advance. Then its violence again put it on the wrong side of the law and of civilized people.

But the Muslim Brotherhood has not gone away. The goal remains: Islamic control of the world.

CHAPTER EIGHT
The Blind Sheik

Introducing Omar Abdel Rahman, the Blind Sheik

Sheik Omar Abdel Rahman (OAR) picked up the flag of Qutb in the seventies (about when Nasser died and was succeeded by Anwar El Sadat).

Sheik Omar Abdel Rahman

He is an *angry man, self-centered and cunning.* He became a scholar, after he graduated from Al-Azhar University in Cairo, the oldest Islamic university in the world. You must have a bachelor's degree, and then get a Master's and a Doctorate in Islam. This is why Omar Abdel Rahman prefers to be called *Dr.* Omar Abdel Rahman. The title carries all his power. (A *fatwa* is an Islamic judgment that should be issued by Islamic Scholars)

Sheik Omar's true color (NY Post)

Also called the Blind Sheik, he is a man who loves to be known. He wants fame, power and money. His interpretation of Islam always benefits his own interest. He wants to be the big leader. A reporter.

Emad S. in a press conference

Once asked him, in front of cameras, if he wanted to be the president of Egypt. A smile lit up his face as he answered, "I would love to be the servant of Egypt."

Dr. Omar Abdel Rahman wished to expand his influence and be the Amir (prince) of Jihad. At first, some Muslims argued that he could not be the Amir, because he is blind. Though some conflicts ensued, but he finally convinced them he was able and capable. He was elected Amir of Jihad.

In being elected Amir of Jihad, he accomplished his goal of being famous, being the leader and having the power. In this capacity, if he issues a fatwa from Egypt or Sudan or an American prison, it has to be followed anywhere in the Muslim world by his followers.

Militant Islamists are around the globe, in every country. They are cells of the Muslim Brotherhood like El Gamaa Al Eslamia. Each cell has its own Amir issuing orders for their followers. They, though, also consult and obey the

Blind Sheik. The various groups work mostly to promote the agenda – Islamic rule - in their home countries. Omar Abdel Rahman usually controls his followers giving them orders and fatwas.

A follower of an Amir will give him a (*Bayah*). A *bayah* is a swearing of allegiance. You hold his hand and kiss it; you bow to him and promise to dedicate your life to him. Once he accepts your pledge, you are obligated to obey him blindly, no questions and no excuses. When a Muslim gives a bayah to his own Amir in his cell, in effect, he also swears his allegiance to the Amir of Jihad, the Blind Sheik – Dr. Omar Abdel Rahman. He is the Amir of Jihad in the entire Muslim world.

The Western press has often talked about Osama Bin Laden or Al Zawahiri issuing a fatwa. This is incorrect. Neither is a scholar with the right or power to issue a fatwa. The orders they give out are not their own. They are obeying and passing on orders from Omar Abdel Rahman or giving their own orders that are not considered fatwas. Omar Abdel Rahman gives all the fatwas in this terrorist fight against the western world. This is why getting rid of Osama Bin Laden does not end terrorism. This is one of those things you didn't know that you didn't know, because the media doesn't know it.

There is also another Egyptian Scholar Yusuf Al Qaradawi who has a long prominent role within the leadership of the Muslim Brotherhood.

Most of Al Qaradawi's views have been controversial in the West; he was refused an entry visa to the United Kingdom in 2008, and barred from entering France in 2012. He is taking partial leadership in the terrorist activity against the west from Qatar where he had political asylum. He is an active supporter of the Blind Sheik.

Manipulation vs. Thinking

Omar Abdel Rahman radicalizes Muslims to become jihadists.

He has a **toolbox:** his words. He is very slick with his words. His skill in manipulation is outstanding.

Emad S. in the back body guarding the Blind Sheik

I heard him speak at a Mosque in Detroit and raise $8K for his purposes in one evening. Just like that. No threats, just convincing words that evoke emotion – his tool box. He captured their minds with his statements. When men do not think for themselves, they fall under the spell of skilled speakers like this one. They are induced to do things they would not do *if they were thinking with their brains.*

As I already stated, it has always been important for me to **think**. It is now more important than ever that individuals think with their own minds. I listen to not just one news outlet. I listen to CNN, FOX, and several other foreign and Arabic sources, and I read. I compare the information, and I evaluate it with my own thinking, using my own knowledge. I can figure out what is actually true and what is a half-truth, a mistruth or a lie. In this way, I protect myself and my country from men like the Blind Sheik.

Thinking is our principle weapon against terrorism.

Omar Abdel Rahman's expanding activities

Though the Muslim Brotherhood got its start in Egypt, the Egyptian government did not approve of this violence in the name of Islam and outlawed the Brotherhood. So Omar Abdel Rahman cunningly changed its name to Tanzim Al Jihad in the 1970's. *Tanzim* means "organization." It soon became

Egyptian Islamic Jihad (EIJ) and then joined up with Al-Gama'a Al-Islamiyya (Islamic Group).

The name changes were meant to hide the Muslim Brotherhood and to confuse people.

Do not be confused. The leader, Dr. Omar Abdel Rahman, has not changed, and the purpose did not change. All of these groups, whatever their names, have one purpose: Islamic rule of the world and the elimination of all non-Muslims.

One of Omar Abdel Rahman's Egyptian recruits was a young ophthalmologist, Dr. Ayman Al Zawahiri.

Dr. Ayman Al Zawahiri

His name is commonly known now in association with al-Qaeda. Khalid Islambouli was another recruit.

With a handful of eager young recruits, Omar Abdel Rahman now needed funding to do his jihad. Money is the name of the game.

North of Cairo is a village called Naj' Hammadi. In 1981, Omar Abdel Rahman issued a fatwa on Coptic Christians who live and work there. Because he wanted their money, he called them infidels based solely on the fact that they were Christians. In response, six Christian goldsmiths were killed, and five kilograms of gold and three thousand Egyptian pounds were stolen. Items matching the description of this loot were found in a package under Omar Abdel Rahman's bed in a raid. He said one of his followers had asked him to keep the package and had put it under his bed. He said he couldn't know what was in it – after all, he is blind!

Coptics in Egypt after the Massacre

There were no repercussions at the time. "We got away with it," Omar Abdel Rahman said to himself. "We killed these people in Naj' Hammadi. We are still alive, and we are more powerful. So let us proceed to our next mission."

About this time, Egyptian President Anwar El Sadat signed a peace agreement with the Jews, the Camp David Accord. Everybody is happy about peace in the Middle East, right?

Camp David Peace Agreement

Not Omar Abdel Rahman. Cooperation with Americans and Jews made Sadat an "infidel", according to him. He issued a fatwa. Khalid Islambouli, a military officer, was chosen to kill Sadat during a parade on October 6, 1981. Islambouli was executed for the crime. Omar Abdel Rahman had been jailed some time earlier in a futile effort by the government to crack down on the violence in Egypt. Still, it was proven that Omar Abdel Rahman issued the fatwa and effectively ordered the killing; but he suffered no penalty.

The Blind Sheik at Sadat's assassination trial

Omar Abdel Rahman eventually was released from prison and placed under house arrest. There were policeman and guards all around the house and even inside it. He was very restricted. Soon tiring of being under house arrest, he asked for a technician to look at his broken washing machine. Before the repairman got to the house, he was captured and replaced by the Blind Sheik's followers. Then they hauled the washer out to be repaired with Omar Abdel Rahman inside. He was slick. Not smart; just slick.

He was taken to Saudi Arabia, and Afghanistan and other places, and finally ended up in Sudan. He ran Al-Gama'a Al-Islamiyya from there for a while, sometimes traveling to other Middle Eastern sites, like Pakistan.

The Blind Sheik in Afghanistan

His right-hand man, Al Zawahiri had been arrested as well. While in prison, he gave press conferences, always keeping the Sheik and his cause in front of the Egyptian public. Once released from prison, he went to England and requested political asylum.

Omar Abdel Rahman's left arm was Osama Bin Laden, at that time a foot soldier in Afghanistan fighting the Russians.

The Russians were still the main enemy of the Americans. The US wanted to help oust them from Afghanistan, where the *mujahidin* were fighting them. The CIA effectively said to Omar Abdel Rahman, "OK, you are the leader of these guys. What do they need to fight the Russians?"

The Blind Sheik answered, "Stingers, shoulder-launched missiles." The CIA provided them, and other help including millions of US dollars, secretly to defeat the Russians. This will come back to haunt the US for many years.

Change of Venue

The Blind Sheik eventually landed in Sudan. It wasn't long before the inconveniences of living in a country wracked by war- War he instigated or encouraged – grew old. He decided to move on, and the United States looked good. Lots of money there, and it was safer.

However, Omar Abdel Rahman was on the list of people not allowed into the USA. He was a known terrorist, linked to acts of world terrorism, and a rebel instigator. Omar Abdel Rahman's cooperation with the US during the Afghan rebellion came in handy.

What should the US Embassy in Sudan do? Why, the answer was clear: immediately issue him a visitor's visa to enter the U.S. While this does not seem to make sense to us in hindsight, the State Department had not used foresight in recruiting or offering help against the Russians. This was the logical result of not thinking about long-term consequences of working with a terrorist.

The U.S. Embassy, on orders from the State department, allowed a known Islamic terrorist to come live in the United States. We have paid a tragic price for that mistake.

The Blind Sheik was more effective from America. America was a stronger platform from which to conduct his war against the Egyptian President Hosni Mubarak. He also felt he would be untouchable in America. And perhaps, in many ways, he was right. During the 2012 elections in Egypt, President Obama's administration allowed Omar Abdel Rahman a fifteen minute phone call from his U.S. prison to Egypt, in which he expressed support for Morsy, who was subsequently elected and tried to institute an Islamist government.

In any case, whether the Feds felt they were repaying favors or whether they were trying to keep the Blind Sheik quiet and under watch, they allowed him to live in the U.S., where, after awhile, he settled in NJ, just outside NYC.

That is where my story crosses his.

Emad S. and the Blind Sheik

CHAPTER NINE
The Blind Sheik in NY

While still working at the hotel, I had started hanging out at the courthouse for the trial of El Sayyid Nosair, for the murder of Rabbi Meir Kahane, a prominent, outspoken leader of the Jewish community.

Sayyid Nosair the Kahane's assassin

Now that I was no longer employed at the hotel Chatwel, I could spend more time information gathering. I listened and watched. I made myself seen and, slowly, recognized.

Emad S. during demonstration (undercover)

I struck up conversations and asked questions. Everything I learned, I took directly back to John Anticev and Louie Napoli or to Nancy Floyd.

Nosair was not convicted of the Rabbi's murder. The jury found him guilty of possession of a firearm and assault. While the surrounding community, especially the Jewish segment, was very angry about his acquittal from the murder charge, the Islamists were angry that there had been any conviction at all.

Emad S. undercover

I spoke as though I were on the side of the Islamists and began to go to the Al Farooque Mosque where the Alkifah Refugee Center or Service Office (MAK) operates, Aboubakr Mosque in Queens, Almomneen Mosque in Brooklyn, and Al Salam Mosque in New Jersey. The center's founder was an Islamic militant from Pakistan named Abdullah Azzam. He has a bunch of these Service Offices set up across the U.S. to raise money for the jihad.

In the course of these visits and meetings, I met the men who followed the Amir of jihad and did his bidding.

These men appeared to be soft-spoken scholars. And they *were* scholars. But "scholar" does not mean to jihadists what it means to westerners. In America, a "scholar" implies a philosopher, one who will address a problem and come up with a peaceful solution that will not offend anyone's sensibilities, someone who is quiet and safe and predictable. So "scholar" was a perfect cover for these men. But as I explained earlier, "scholar" meant they were well trained in Islam and had the power to issue fatwa.

This is another example of America not understanding her enemies.

One example of the propensity to violence stands out, a situation I was able to shed light upon much later while going through some files after my work with the FBI was done.

A Muslim Imam in Al Farooque Mosque had been murdered, and his killing remained unsolved.

Judge, Jury, Executioner

A year or so before I came on the scene, there was a discussion about how great sums of money raised at Al Farooque Mosque should be distributed. The money had been raised to help oust the Russians from Afghanistan. But that conflict was settled, and Omar Abdel Rahman felt the funds should go toward other militant causes, such as Egypt. He wanted to overthrow yet another Egyptian leader, Hosni Mubarak.

Mostafa Shalaby argued that since the one million dollars had been raised specifically for Afghanistan, it should still go there. However, the Blind Sheik said, "No. I am the Amir. I am here now. I distribute this money in the way that I think is appropriate for jihad such as Egypt."

Mostafa Shalaby, who was actually in possession of the money as the operator of the Refugee Center, was faithful to his own sheik, Abdullah Azzam.

Shalaby refused to hand over the funds. Rodney Hampton-El, usually called "Dr. Rashid," pressured him for it.

Hampton – El (Dr. Rashid)

Dr. Rashid was a Black Muslim working as an X-Ray technician and known for being a big supporter to the Blind Sheik Omar Abdel Rahman. Shalaby stood up to him. "No. It was raised for Afghanistan. It has to go to that because that's what it's for."

The argument continued, and Shalaby said he would speak to the Blind Sheik about it. Rashid was livid, shouting, "You'll see the Sheik over my dead body!"

So Omar Abdel Rahman, Rodney Hampton-El/Dr. Rashid, and others (the information I gathered points to Mahmud Abouhalima being present with Mohamed Salama and Bilal El Kezy) set up a meeting with Shalaby. His wife Zeinab and kids were sent away to Egypt before the meeting. In Zeinab's words, spoken to me later in a long conversation, "[The Sheik and his men] came to the house, Held a trial for her husband and the next thing she knew, her husband was killed."

Hampton-El told me that, "he was put on trial. And he was found disobedient to the Amir. The Sheik said his blood was permissible." He was shot with a .22 caliber.

Then, according, to Hampton-El, that "he was cut and stabbed and moved upstairs to make it look like the Jews did it for revenge." This murder was not officially solved at the time, but Shalaby had red hair in his hand, and Abouhalima's hair and beard are red.

Then a few years later as I went through some of my old files, I saw this mention of the .22 caliber. I reached out to (Peter Lance) an investigative reporter who wrote so many books about terrorism and the FBI, such as "Triple Cross", "Thousand Years for Revenge" and "The Cover-up".

Peter Lance

I was working with him at the time on an article for play boy magazine. Peter Lance introduced me to Jim Moss, an NYPD detective homicide division in South Brooklyn.

Article in Play Boy Magazine

Detective Jim Moss reopened the case and was clever enough to solve it after 20 years of being a cold case

Detective Jim Moss

In a short time, Azzam and his sons were also killed. They were on their way to prayers when a car bomb went off. It makes sense to me that this, too, was the Sheik's fatwa. It's how he gets rid of people who are in his way.

CHAPTER TEN
Inside

Asset or Informant?

The Feds gather information from many sources. Persons who bring them news, warnings, any information, however large or small, are "informants. The FBI takes what the informant brings them and from that finds probable cause for searches, taps, etc. Those, then, become the evidence used in trials.

An "asset" is a person placed by the authorities for the purpose of gathering intelligence.

I was functioning as an asset. This worked well for me because I had family in Egypt still, and I had my wife and kids here in America with me. I did not wish to put them in any danger.

Emad S. undercover

A Good Cover

The men I met with knew that I had been in the Egyptian military. As for my activities since coming to the US, I presented myself, as a private investigator and a jeweler.

Before I worked at the hotel in Manhattan, I worked for a private investigation/security company in the area of Canal Street, Graham Knowles Associates.

Emad S. as P.I. at Graham Knowles Associates

Though I didn't personally have a P.I. license, I was bonded by the firm's license and could practice under the auspices of the firm. We used a lot of surveillance cameras in our work. Once a client had us install a camera in a car that she and her husband both used. She thought he was cheating on her. Sure enough, he was having an affair with a man. We caught it on tape.

In another instance, a dentist's office that used platinum for fillings found a sizeable quantity missing. After dusting for fingerprints, the police couldn't find the culprit. They called on us. We installed a camera in a speaker to watch the safe. We caught a female employee removing something from the safe and hiding it in her pants. We were watching live feed, so we called the dentist's office and they caught her with the platinum.

My boss and I were experienced with taping and the use of radios and back up. Sometimes we learn as much from what goes wrong as from what goes right. My boss was tailing someone who caught him. He had not kept his radio close at hand, and I was not close enough to get to him in time. He was badly beaten. One punch in his eye put so much pressure on his brain that he suffered stroke-like brain damage and had to close the P.I. practice.

Surveillance was familiar to me, and this knowledge as well as my degree in Electronic Engineering from my military years prepared me for the work that I would now do to help save American lives.

It also served as a cover for me if I showed up with surveillance equipment, cameras, recorders, etc. They were for "my work."

And the jewelry business gave me a cover for the money that I sometimes spent. Both these occupations also explained my free schedule. I was available at odd hours of the day and night for days on end, to cover five mosques between Brooklyn, Queens, and New Jersey is a task that needs a lot of hours.

I spent the days with the Islamist group, and I met with one of the agents, usually Nancy Floyd, at a TGI Friday restaurant to debrief. Because I didn't wear a wire, I had to tell the Feds what I knew often, so I wouldn't forget it, because I took notes in my head.

In a relatively short time, I gained the trust of the cell.

The Action Begins

One time I was asked to drive the Sheik and some of the men to Detroit for a fund raising event at the mosque there. It was amazing to watch his persuasion, his manipulation. He used words to provoke the men gathered in the mosque for prayers.

"You Muslim people are living here in America worshipping the mighty dollar, yet your sisters and mothers are pregnant with blue-eyed fetuses in the Arab world. How dare you let your sisters be screwed by American soldiers in Arab lands, screwing your mothers and sisters while you are here worshipping the mighty dollar." He knows how to press buttons and provoke their manhood.

The mosque was one hundred percent full, and people stood outside around it to hear the Blind Sheik speak. He was able to plant that picture in all their minds – their women back in the Arab world pregnant with blue-eyed babies. His message was that the Americans were an occupying military, occupying the Holy Land, sinning with Muslim women, while these men were here getting rich.

Immediately, everybody pulled out their almighty dollars. I was one of the people who sat and counted the money at the end of the evening. And that day I counted, in my hand alone, $8,000 in one hour in that mosque.

But more importantly, in that one lecture, he left 1,000 people walking out ready to kill any American they met. This is how people become terrorists. [1]

---

1   Look at Abdulmutallab, the Nigerian kid who got on a flight with a bomb in his underwear. He was a depressed little kid, until Anwar al-Awlaki, a radical Imam, came along and with a good "toolbox" and provoked his manhood and used his religious belief to send him to kill "infidels." Of the 300 people on the plane, there are no infidels, unless maybe a few are atheists. They are believers. And this kid doesn't know that.

He said in court, "Mujahidin are proud to kill in the name of God. And that is exactly what God told us to do in the Quran... Today is a day of victory." The radical had manipulated him and twisted the Quran. Consider Major Hassan at the Fort Hood Massacre. When he started to shoot, Major Hassan shouted, "Allahu Akhbar!" (God is Great) as he began shooting people who were not infidels. The victims' families and friends went to church to pray for them, so they were believers. Hassan did not know this. Interestingly, Mr. Hassan also sat under the teaching of Anwar al-Awlaki, the radical who influenced the young man from Nigeria.

I am angry about the way my religion has been distorted and perverted to mean violence. This is why I like to quote the Quran against terrorism. The Quran teaches tolerance. God said, "I created the human race, different tribes and different populations to recognize each other." Dark eyed people, blue eyed people; dark skinned with light skinned; blond hair with baldheads. God taught us tolerance when he instructed the Prophet Mohammed (PBUH) to marry a Christian woman and a Jewish woman for the purpose of teaching us it's ok to marry a Jew or a Christian.

God's greatness is in putting many tribes and many different believers together in one place who tolerate each other. Sheik Omar Abdel Rahman knows this, but he will not approach the subject. It goes against his agenda

The van we took to Detroit had been rented by and rigged by the FBI.

The Sheik, of course, didn't know this. As I had presented myself as a Jeweler, he thought I was wealthy. So he asked me if I would rent a van for him and some of his men to go on this trip. "Of course," I answered. And I went straight to the FBI.

They provided me with a van and wired it to record the trip. At that time, recording was done on tapes, and no tape was long enough to get the whole eight-hour trip. So a high tech recording method was set up in the van. However, it was an analog touchy system, highly technical and difficult to install properly.

The day we were to leave for the trip, I got the call that the van was ready. I and several of the Sheik's men got in my car and drove to the pickup site where I told them I had left the van. It was actually right near 26 Federal Plaza. But as we were on our way, my phone rang.

I always pretended it was my wife if the agents called me when I was with the cell.

"Hi Honey. How are you?"

"Don't come yet. There's been an issue with the recording equipment, and we need a few minutes to fix it."

"Ok, Honey. No problem. I'll take care of it for you." A few minutes passed, and I headed once again for the pick-up point. Again the phone rang.

"Yes, Honey?"

"No, no, don't come yet."

"Oh Honey, just don't worry about it. It will be ok." And then to the guys in the car: "Do you mind if we pick up a sandwich at a place I know before we get the van?"

After yet another call and delay, I was allowed to pick up the van with assurances that all was now set and working properly. I already had a set of van keys, so we picked up the Sheik and the others and headed for Detroit with me driving.

On the way, the Sheik asked some personal questions of me. Where was I from? What had I done in the military? How many years? etc. He wondered if I knew about bomb making and high-powered explosives. I said I did. He asked if I knew about guns and if I could shoot.

"Yes. I was a sharpshooter."

He surprised me by saying, "You know you were not a good Muslim the whole time you were working for that government?"

I allowed my surprise to show. "I wasn't? Why?"

"Because Hosni Mubarak is an infidel who rules without Islamic law, and the whole time you were serving him in the military you were serving an infidel."

"Oh, my God!" I cried. "Don't tell me that! I thought I was doing a good thing. Now what should I do?" I feigned distress, though I really was excited, sensing something was coming. However, I couldn't have guessed what it was.

"You can be forgiven if you do an act of penance. You can earn forgiveness if you turn your rifle against Hosni Mubarak and shoot him. Kill the infidel. He is coming to New York next week on a visit. Do it then. That will be your repentance."

I don't have to tell you I was shocked inside, but of course I did not show that. I said, "Of course, that is no problem. Definitely, yes."

The president of Egypt would come next week to NY, and I was supposed to assassinate him. To say I was worried is an understatement. I couldn't know if others from the group might have gotten the same orders, so even if I didn't do it, I couldn't be sure someone else wouldn't do it, like Ali Mohamed he was a former Egyptian Military officer with radical views. Then we would have an assassinated Egyptian President on our hands, on American soil!

As soon as I got home, I called my friend in Egyptian Intelligence and told him. Low and behold, they cancelled the president's visit. Of course, I told the FBI agents I had called my friend in Egypt. But I knew they would hear the whole damning conversation with the Sheik on the tapes. We had him!

Only the tapes didn't work. We got back from Detroit, with me quite satisfied with the solid evidence, what we had gotten; and then they told me the recording method had not worked.

All that delay, all that driving around, dangerously making up excuses to not go get the van right away while the technicians tried to repair the recording system... for nothing. It was my word alone.

When we would come to the Blind Sheik's trial much later, Andrew McCarthy, the prosecutor, would put me on the stand and question me about this ordered assassination. It all would depend on if the jury would believe my word or not, Future recordings, fortunately, would corroborate this story. There are many other recordings of speeches by the Blind Sheik calling Hosni Mubarak a "loyal dog to America," saying he is an infidel and should be killed. This made it believable to the jury that the Blind Sheik would ask me to actually carry out the killing. Also, they knew the Blind Sheik had ordered the assassination of President Anwar El Sadat.

But in the beginning it was only my word, because the FBI's apparatus did not function in this incident.

CHAPTER ELEVEN
Bomb Building

I had presented myself as a bomb expert. I wasn't, but I knew something about explosives, of course. After the trip to Detroit, my attitude was something like, "OK guys, I just retired from eighteen years of military service in Egypt. I used to be in the weapons and bomb division in the military. By helping these infidels in government, I was being sinful. I'm trying to repent."

Mixing the witch's Brew

I went along with Ibrahim El Gabrowny a few times to visit his cousin Nosair in prison after his conviction.

Ibrahim El Gabrowny

At first he was at Riker's Island. Then he was transferred to Attica Correctional Facility. Between them, they started talking about building bombs to get revenge for Nosair's imprisonment. They asked me to build twelve pipe bombs to target synagogues around New York. Also in their sights were Judge Alvin Schlesinger, who presided in Nosair's trial, and Dov Hikind, the Assemblyman for the Jewish section of New York, who loudly protested Nosair's acquittal for the murder of Rabbi Kahane. (He was later convicted of it in conjunction with another charge against him.)

Where would I get the pipes and the powder to make bombs? I told them I would need materials. Ibrahim talked to Ali El Shinawy about the components.

Ali El Shinawy

El-Shinawy was another Egyptian and on the board of the Abou bakr mosque in Queens. He got in touch with me.

"Ok, Brother Emad. Tell me what you need. I'm ready to help."

I said first of all we needed pipes. He said he had a plumber who could provide the pipes and thread them for us. He would also supply caps for the pipes. Ali El Shinawy also suggested that I have to carry a gun just in case if the FBI approaches us we can defend ourselves, I told him I don't know where to get a gun from. Ali El Shinawy stuck his hand into his vest and handed me a gun and he said you can give me $50 later on. I thanked him and I called John and Louie urgently to show them the gun. It was a problem to leave the gun in working conditions with their undercover operative so they took the gun to the FBI lab who disabled the gun and returned it to me just in case if Ali El Shinawy will ask me about it again.

Ibrahim El Gabrowny brought me powder. It was in cartridges that he used in his nail gun in his day job as a contractor. But it was such a small amount; there was no way to make it set off pipe bombs. So they talked to Saddiq, who made arrangements with his friends in Pennsylvania. One night we drove all the way from New York into Pennsylvania to pick up two boxes of dynamite.

The Feds went with us that night, though my friends from the cell didn't know it, of course. All these movements were monitored. Unfortunately – or fortunately, perhaps, there was some confusion, and the dynamite was not ready for us. We drove all the way back empty handed.

I eventually suggested to El Gabrowny and El Shinawy that the timing was bad for these synagogue bombs and that they would be counterproductive to other operations in the works. Convinced, they discontinued the plan.

But meanwhile, when I bought the fuse for the bomb, my handlers passed that information to their superior, Assistant Special Agent in Charge, Carson Dunbar. He decided he needed me to wear a wire and become an "Informant."

Trouble Brewing

Dunbar sent one of his senior men, John Crouthamel, to meet me and resolve this issue of my wearing a wire. I had refused to do so. If I wore a wire and gathered incriminating evidence, it could be used directly in court. In that case, I would have to personally appear in court to testify and become an informant. My family, both in the US and in Egypt, and I would be in danger.

Crouthamel, Anticev, Napoli, and I met in a hotel room in Manhattan which was arranged by Nancy Floyd. Crouthamel tried to convince me to wear the wire. I continued to refuse.

Nancy, who was still with the Russian section and not actually with JTTF, was asked to leave the room. When she was gone, John Crouthamel made it obvious how crude he was.

"We have to get that bitch off this case," he said. It was a turf war, showing the jealousy between departments. No department wanted an agent from another section handling their assets.

However, Nancy was a professional, smart young lady who put her life on the line for her country on a regular basis. She was one of the two smartest women I ever met, along with my cousin Eman. I had great, great respect for Nancy. She was professional; she knew what she was doing and had respect for those with whom she worked. I had been working with her for many months by this time. She showed me respect, and I trusted her. I had not built any trust with Crouthamel nor with his boss Dunbar. My loyalty lay with Nancy.

I saw no reason for Crouthamel to say what he did, other than a character flaw in him. Crouthamel had no understanding of or respect for my work with Nancy and the professional relationship we had. He had no understanding of my sense of loyalty. His comment caused me to distrust him even more. (What he didn't know did hurt him.)

He then added insult to injury by asking, "Ok, how much do you want?"

"What?!"

"How much do you want to be paid to testify?" For nine months I helped the Russian squad, the INS, the JTTF – and I did not get paid one iota. Not one penny. I did not expect to get paid. On the contrary, when I took the agents to lunch, I acted like a Middle Eastern gentleman and paid for the bill. I did not expect to be paid for helping my America. I just wanted to be helpful and of use.

He thought I was holding out for cash. I was offended and insulted. All these weeks and months I had been working for free. I hadn't suggested getting anything else for my work and for the danger I ran.

He was calling me a money hungry son of a bitch. I was not.

"Excuse me? Do I really look that low in your vision for you to treat me this way?" I grabbed my jacket and headed for the door.

John Anticev interceded. "Wait, wait. Slow down." I didn't leave, but I wasn't giving in, either.

I refused to work with John Crouthamel after that.

CHAPTER TWELVE
Distrust and Insult

The FBI Tug of War

There are two kinds of FBI agents, and the division between them is clear.

The "Suits" sit in air-conditioned offices. They have nice desks and eat good food. They put their feet up on tables and make decisions.

The "Humps" are the agents who go out in the street and do the work. They eat shit and sweat and get cold and work in the rain and snow to make the cases. The Humps on the street, rain or shine, cold or hot, are bombarded by the abuse and misuse of American Liberty.

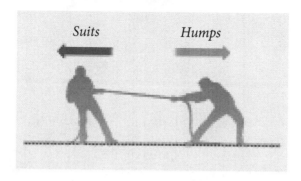

The Suits, in their offices, are often completely disconnected from what the Humps are gathering, building and executing. All it takes is one stroke from a Suit's pen to destroy the effort of the Humps. The sweat and tears they shed evaporates due to the Suit's lack of knowledge, understanding, and connection to the street. It seems to me that the higher in management one goes, the more apparent the separation between the two, but thank GOD that was then, I noticed lately during my tour and speeches to some terrorist task forces around the country that the humps became suits and that made a huge difference in the communication between them. It would take pages to recount the incidents when some of the Suits I came in contact with from 1991 to 1995 showed ignorance or lack of understanding of the work their agents and I did every day, of the danger we were in. I think many were appointed to their positions only for political reasons, and much of what they did or decided had administrative decisions and very disconnected from the investigative work.

A few notable exceptions exist. Louis Frey was one of the most successful, ethical and dedicated Directors of the FBI that is because one day, he was also a Hump. He walked the walk and talked the talk of the Agents on the street, before he became the Director of the FBI

The ASAC (Assistant Special Agent in Charge) of the Russian Squad, Len Predtechenskis, was very successful in running his Squad. He, too, was a Hump before he became a Suit.

Humps

My first contact with the FBI was in 1991, when I was approached by a professional, ethical and dedicated Hump, Nancy Floyd. She didn't work 9:00 to 5:00. Her life revolved around her career as an agent for the Russian Squad in the New York office. Sharp as a razor, she approached me, identifying her self and showing me her credentials. She quickly earned my trust by her straightforwardness. I felt useful but she never made me feel that I was being *used*. The courtesy and appreciation she showed me, in the duration of my work with her, and her intelligence and dedication painted a great picture of a female FBI agent in a world dominated by males.

John Anticev, FBI, and Louie Napoli, NYPD, were both Humps on the JTTF. Steve Vierra was the FBI "bomb expert" in our group. They worked hard and often had to find solutions or change plans on the street to save my skin and protect our operation. While the work we did was not pleasurable, making the acquaintance of these four and working with them, and others who came and went in our mission, certainly was an honor.

These four were my contacts, and handlers for the first months I worked undercover in New York.

Suits

My shocking experience with the Suits had started when the JTTF Supervisor Crouthamel requested me to change my role from intelligence asset to informant. I was insulted, humiliated and belittled in a hotel room where the meetings took place. I refused to work with John Crouthamel, the supervisor, who acted like God's deputy on earth.

Furthermore, I was amazed and astonished when I met with Crouthamel's supervisor in the New York office, Carson Dunbar, who was in charge of the Joint Terrorist Task Force. That is when I experienced the complete separation between the Humps and the Suits.

Carson Dunbar had not met me yet when he decided I should wear a wire. He was one of the Assistant Special Agent in Charge (ASAC) in the New York office, and he wanted to see me himself. He decided he wanted me brought into his office in 26 Federal Plaza in Manhattan which is the craziest idea ever to bring an undercover operative to the FBI building to meet an ASAC. The agents had to take extreme measures by using unmarked cars into the back streets to meet with their undercover operative so he is not compromised, yet the ASAC decides to bring me to his office. I think this decision was made because he never trusted his agents.

I had proven my worth and loyalty already with the evidence and the corroborated information I had given the FBI. The work I had been doing for nine months with Nancy Floyd and with these agents seemed to count for nothing. He did not trust me, and this caused me to begin to distrust him, too. (I heard through the grape vine that he never even looked at my file before I came in. He did not bother to find out all that I had already done to help the agency.)

Still, I was not an agent, and I was of foreign origin, though I was an American who loved my country. I could maybe understand having some hesitancy towards me, just a cautious need to be sure of me.

But my God, trust your own people! Dunbar seemed to think his own agents couldn't handle me or what I brought them. Combined with what I would see over the next weeks, convinces me of his lack of confidence in his people. John Anticev, a banker-turned-FBI agent, and Louie Napoli, a veteran detective with the NYPD, my official JTTF handlers, were his men and had proven their abilities and trustworthiness. He had to prove something else, I suppose.

Windows and Mirrors

First Lieutenant Emad S.

As a former commander, I had been the leader of over a thousand men.

Emad S. with his soldiers

I had a theory about leadership called "Windows and Mirrors." When I lead my men, I assigned their duties, and I allowed them to act, expecting them to perform at their best. If they did well, I looked out the "window" to them and praised their work and dedication. If they failed, I looked in the "mirror" and wondered where I had gone wrong and what I must do to enable my men to complete their duties correctly. I gave praise for work well done, and I accepted the responsibility for failures. I did not interfere with them when they were doing a good job or try to get control of or credit for their accomplishments.

It seemed to me, Carson Dunbar did not share my philosophy. He seemed to distrust his people to do their work. Or perhaps he sensed things were getting bigger and he wanted the credit.

I know he wanted Nancy Floyd off the case. She technically wasn't under his supervision. Apparently, the FBI did not like having this crossover of handlers and information between sections. I think he also resented Nancy because she was a woman. That was my impression.

Meeting Carson Dunbar

An undercover informant coming in to the headquarters was highly unusual and extremely dangerous, both to me and to the operation. I was doing intelligence on people who were working everywhere in New York City. Some worked for the telephone company; some worked for the City. Nossair had been a worker in the city of New York. If somebody saw me going up and down at the FBI's New York office, I'd be dead meat. Yet he insisted I be brought to Federal Plaza.

I appreciate the way John Anticev and Louie Napoli brought me. They were smart. They got me into a black limo and drove to the bottom garage of 26 Federal, then opened the door right in front of the elevator, made sure it was empty, and whisked me straight to the 28th floor. That way I'd be seen only by agents.

Louie and John, Nancy Floyd, Crouthamel, and Steve Vierra were present. The agents all walked into Dunbar's office and stood in a line with their hands crossed in front of them. I understand this. He is their boss. He is not MY boss.

Bad Start

I'm a retired military commander. I led thousands of people. When I walked into my general's office, I stood at attention. But Dunbar is not my general and does not outrank me. I am an American citizen, not an FBI agent.

Before I sat down, I shook his hand. He was surprised and hesitant, like I'm a piece of crap, and he wanted to remove his royal hand from mine as fast as he could. I think he expected me to stand way back by the door and address him by "Yes sir," like his agents. He thought I would bow my head and cross my hands in front of my belly and come to him as a third class citizen from a Middle Eastern country.

His attitude evoked a similar response in me, toward him. I grabbed a chair, pulled it up across from his desk, and sat down.

He dismissed the agents and pulled a chair around. He propped up his feet right toward me, and I couldn't help but notice his expensive Italian shoes.

I was dressed appropriately for this meeting – suit and tie. But nothing expensive, I had a family to feed.

Carson Dunbar dressed very well, and I can respect that. But I know something about intimidation and how to use it. I understood the Italian shoes in my face were exactly that – an attempt to intimidate me into doing what he ordered. It was his way of saying he was better than me. That act of extending the feet in that way is the maximum insult to a Middle Eastern proud man. I don't know if he knew this or not.

Because I am familiar with such methods, and because I do not bow to any man, only to God, this action put a distance between us right from the start. It backfired on him. Instead of treating me with respect, he treated me as below him. He ruined any chance he had of convincing me to do as he wished.

He started the conversation with, "They tell me that [the bad guys] are trying to get you to build bombs."

"Yes."

"I have instructed them to put you on the box." He referred to the polygraph test.

"I've been working with Nancy for nine months, delivering this information, and all of a sudden you want to put me on a polygraph?"

"Yes. It's getting serious now. You're talking about building bombs."

"The box is not going to work because I know how to manipulate a polygraph"

But he pushed it. "No. Tomorrow you come back, and we put you on the polygraph."

Polygraph

The next day, Nancy drove me back to 26 Federal Plaza, and Louie Napoli and John Anticev took me to the polygraph examiner, a nice guy. I explained to him. "I don't think you'll be able to have a conclusive exam, because I've beaten the box before. I don't allow anybody to go inside my mind."

I mentioned already that I like the word "Think." You should be loyal to your own brain. I don't think it's appropriate for anyone to penetrate my brain unless I allow it.

I had never been an intelligence officer, but I took security courses. When you are a commander, you have to secure your people. Part of security is putting your people on the polygraph and learning how polygraph manipulation can happen.

The guy put me on the box, asked the questions, and said, "Thank you. The exam is finished." I left the room, and he delivered the results: inconclusive.

Carson Dunbar's reaction: "We'll do it again."

I did it again. Different examiner; same result. Dunbar's frustration was increasing. He decided to take me to New Jersey to meet a polygraph tech they brought in from Washington, D.C. His name was Jack DeMarco. He was supposed to be The Guy, the one who knew how to do this better than anyone else.

By this third exam, I was starting to get pissed off. They were creating more and more distrust in me. They were increasing the gap between me and the agents I worked with.

Where were these exams when I was delivering information every day for the last nine months?

The third tester approached me very aggressively. "It's my understanding you've been on the box twice before?"

"Yes."

"Well they make mistakes. These are the people I taught, and sometimes they do make mistakes. But I'm the head of the polygraph unit in Washington. I don't make mistakes." He was rather arrogant.

"Oh, really? You don't make mistakes?"

"No."

"Ok. Try me." I rubbed him the wrong way with that answer.

He said, "Really?"

"Yes."

"Try this." He took a long piece of paper and wrote the numbers one through ten on it. He stuck it on the wall and sat me in a chair facing it. He told me to pick a number but to not tell him; just write it on a slip of paper and put it in my pocket. I did so.

"Now I'm going to ask you, 'Did you pick number one?' Then you answer, 'No.' I'll ask you for all ten numbers, and you always answer, 'No.' When we get to the number you picked, I'll tell you."

He did this. I always said, "No."

At the end, he hesitated and said, "Uhhh…you picked either five or six."

I made a sound like a game show buzzer when the contestant gets the wrong answer. I was being a smart ass. He asked, "What was the number you chose?"

"Oh, you want me to tell you the number I chose. It was four."

"Ok. How did you do that?"

I said, "Now sit down, let me tell you how…" That rubbed him very wrong.

This is not how polygraphs are usually conducted. In the past, the tester always tried to make me feel at ease. You want the subject to be calm so you get reactions if he lies. You don't want him upset and angry to start establishing the base line of the subject. Then you can tell what is the reaction to the questions.

After setting me up with this aggression and games, he proceeded to ask me questions. But they weren't questions in connection to my work with the New York cell, the purpose for this test in the first place. Instead, they were about my connections with Egypt. He seemed to be trying to make me out as a spy for Egypt! What did this have to do with Nosair's bomb? How did this help us in our supposed common goal?

His report on the test was "inconclusive"

To Dunbar, however, he wrote, "Deceptive." I still do not know why that result was changed after he went back to Washington. I see no value in discrediting me, the only inside eyes and ears they had in the NY jihadist cell, at a time when bomb building was happening! Any explanation is very troubling. Was the Sheik being protected? Did they not want a case against the Islamists? I still do not know, though I have my suspicions.

And I'm Out

Dunbar called me back to his office after he got the test results. I bought myself some expensive Italian shoes for this visit. I can put on suits and ties as well. I showed I was not intimidated. Let us not play that game if we are to work together; that was my thinking.

He came around his desk again and sat in a chair. But this time, he reached down and took off his expensive Italian shoes. I don't know if he had noticed my shoes or if this was an intentional insult again or something else. Then he crossed his legs under him and sat on them. This created a distance from me.

I agree he should be doubtful and secure his people, check them out. Have doubts. Be certain.

But playing spiffy, and sticking his shoes in my face, the lack of trust with the "box, - and the box, and the box again – I was insulted. I was cooperating with the FBI by my own choice as a good citizen. Even if I had broken English, I was an American citizen. I had achieved my dream of coming to America, to make a way for myself, to care for my children and give them the opportunity of an education in the best country in the world. But I was risking it all for my country. I had no obligation to do so. I owed the FBI nothing.

But I love this country more than anything else. I just wanted to be of use in protecting it and cleaning up the terrorists roaming the streets, threatening our American way of life.

Don't insult a guy who is not gaining a penny from all this wasted time, coming to your office, which is dangerous. Go corroborate what I gave you, yes, and don't treat your own agents like they are nothing.

So anyway, he took his fancy shoes off and sat cross-legged. He looked at me and said, "Now you've GOT to wear a wire."

"No. I will not. When I started to work for Nancy, I told her I don't want to jeopardize my sister, my uncles. They live in Egypt. The Blind Sheik's followers are all over Egypt. I was told if I wear a wire, I have to testify."

"Yes. You would."

"No. But here is what I WILL do. Look, I would wear a wire in Attica when I visit Nosair again. That will prove what he is saying. But don't use it in court; let me keep it. Use it to go get probable cause search warrants and things so you can get the evidence without me."

My record spoke for itself. I had brought important information forward already that had proven to be true. He just didn't trust me, especially after those polygraphs. He didn't trust anybody, really, I don't think. If I wore a wire to Attica, he would know that what I was reporting was true and could trust me.

I had already thought about this option. I had constructed a series of open-ended questions to ask Nosair. I always used open-ended questions to avoid entrapping anyone. John Anticev, Nancy and louie had helped me understand the legal system in America, so I was always careful with my questions. You cannot say to him, "Let's build a bomb." That would be entrapment, because you cannot suggest.

I told Dunbar that this was my plan, what I intended to do at that time I didn't fully understand how the criminal legal system worked but he could've explained it to me instead he put his face close to mine. "You Middle Eastern, coming to this country, dragging sand in your shoes, thinking you're going to tell me how to do my job?"

""I am respectful to everybody. I expect them to be respectful to me, especially since I am here trying to help you do your job.

"Carson," (he didn't like that!) "I am here to help you do your job. You cannot do this job without somebody like me.

"Yes, I'm telling you how to do it because you don't know how. I am in the Sheik's cell, all the way into El Sayyid Nosair's cell. And this is what you couldn't do. Neither you nor your agents could get close to these people.

"And these people are going to blow up bombs in Manhattan – in my America! So if I can do it, and you don't know how, then you'd listen to me."

" Get out of my office!"

And I walked out. Insulted.

I left that room and I said to Nancy Floyd, Anticev and Napoli, who were waiting outside, "Dunbar is treating me like a Middle Eastern sonovabitch coming from Egypt, dragging sand in my shoes and trying to run the FBI. And I don't like it.

"Don't call me when the bomb goes off."

The Inevitable

February 26, 1993 12:17 p.m.
North Tower of the World Trade Center is bombed.
6 people were killed, one of them was pregnant; 1,000 injured
$8 billion dollars of destruction

Whose fault was this?
Who was responsible?
Who didn't follow through?
Who dropped the ball?
Who screwed up?
Who will be accountable?

Who?
This was NOT inevitable. But unfortunately <u>*accountability*</u>
is something we never have in America.

Who was held accountable for the 1993 WTC bombing?
Who was held accountable for 9/11?
Who was held accountable for the Underwear bomber?
Who was held accountable for the Fort Hood Massacre?
Who was held accountable for the Time Square bomber?
Who was held accountable for the Boston Marathon bombing?
Who was held accountable for the Benghazi incident?

PART II

"Emad Salem is one of the bravest men I've ever known. He was a breathtakingly effective confidential informant. Many, many people in New York City are alive today because of his heroism. He was as good a witness as I ever put on the stand or heard testify during twenty-five years of [trials]. He is also beyond a doubt the strangest, wiliest, most impossible, most infuriating pain in the ass I ever will know if I live to be a thousand."

--Andrew McCarthy, *Willful Blindness*[2]

---

2   McCarthy, Andrew C. Willful Blindness, p.137. Encounter Books, NY, N, 2008.

CHAPTER THIRTEEN
Round Two

Andrew McCarthy was an outstanding federal prosecutor. He treated me with respect and helped me in every way he could to understand how the cookie crumbles. He tried to make sure others didn't hurt me. But he said the above about me. Why? Why would he say that?

Why was I a "pain the ass"? Here's why.

Suspicion

After the WTC bombing in 1993, James Fox, the Deputy Director of the New York Office, held a press conference. One reporter asked him a very interesting question. It went something like this: "We hear you had a mole in the bombing cell. Didn't your informant give you any warning about this?"

James Fox should have been surprised at this question. Wondering how this information was leaked. His response might have been, "We had no informant in the cell and so could not have known this was happening."

Instead, his answer was along the lines of: "The informant gave us nothing, no warning." No denial of a mole, which would have protected me if I had still been inside.

In fact, his answer affirmed that they did, indeed, have an inside guy, when in truth they did not. They had taken me out some months earlier without having a plan B to follow up on the potential bomb-building cell. Covered their asses, but carefully and purposefully left mine out in the wind. I had to wonder.

I had to wonder how the press would have gotten any idea that I was working in the cell in the first place. The only way was a leak somewhere. Did the FBI leak it on purpose? Did the CIA find out?

That leak could only result in my death. Why would the Feds want me dead? Maybe because I was the only one outside the JTTF who could reveal the massive FBI shortcomings that led to these six deaths and one thousand injuries. Maybe because the CIA needed to protect their guy, the Blind Sheik?. Either way couldn't end well for me.

I *did* wonder, though, why James Fox had said I had given the FBI no information.

FBI Deputy Director James Fox

How embarrassing for the FBI to say, "Yes, we knew a bomb was about to be built." Then how would they explain why they hadn't followed up? How would they explain that they drove out their main asset in this fight on terrorism because of Dunbar's arrogance and stubbornness? I can see it now: "Uh, well, yes, we did have an asset, but he offended Carson Dunbar's pride and made him feel less than all-knowing, so the ASAC kicked him out and left us without any inside ears or eyes, so we couldn't tell if the bomb was being built or not or when the bomb would go off. And really, six lives and billions of dollars isn't too high a price to pay for the Dunbar's self-image, is it?" Sure.

I knew then, for sure, my life was in danger from within the circle of the "good guys."

Adding to this perception, when I came into the FBI headquarters for the first time after the 1993 WTC bombing, what was the first thing I saw? A big board with pictures of the suspects. Oh yes, they had the pictures. They knew all these guys before it ever happened. But guess who was at the top of the board?

Yours truly.

They had me at the top of the suspect list. When I questioned my picture being there, I was told something like, "Oh, no, that was a mistake. Sorry, sorry." And they took it down.

Mahmoud Abouhalima   *Mohamed Abouhalima*

I asked John Anticev are you guys watching these people?

"Yes we have surveillance eyeballing Mahmoud Abouhalima."

"Impossible"

"Why?"

"Mahmoud is out of the country"

"What?"

"He is under arrest in Egypt and if you don't hurry up and bring him back he could be killed and you will never be able to get your guy."

"When did that happen?"

"After the bombing he went to Saudi Arabia for Omra, then he went to his mother's house in Egypt where he was picked up by the Egyptian feds, your surveillance is watching his brother Mohamed Abouhalima."

John Anticev trusted my information and immediately acted upon it.

I think he was happy to have me back so he can see and hear what is going on inside the cell again.

Mahmoud Abouhalima after the arrest by John Anticev on the right and Louie Napolie on the left

A special plane and special mission went to Egypt to bring Mahmoud Abouhalima back to stand a trail.

But I knew then that as much as I might like John Anticev or Louie Napoli, the only person I could count on was... GOD and myself.

Carson Dunbar or someone involved with the polygraph had tried to make me out to be an Egyptian spy just a few months earlier. Now with my picture as a suspect, I was afraid. Full of fear. Full of uncertainty. Angry. Very angry. The anger and distrust about my position in the eyes of the Bureau would not leave me in all the long months to come. It would nearly kill me at one point.

I was angry at what had been done to me. But I was angrier at what had been done to six people, now dead, and their families on Feb. 26. To over one thousand people suffering injuries. Their lives changed forever at noon that day. And it could have been prevented. It could have been stopped.

I think I could have stopped it.

My own guilt made me the angriest. If I had not been so adamant about not wearing a wire, they would have had the hard evidence to prevent the bombing.

If I had been able to convince Carson Dunbar to let me remain an as an asset instead of an informant.

If, if, if...

And that's why I came back in. I knew when I did that I would have to wear a wire, drop my American dream, my identity, my credentials, and put my family in Egypt and in American myself included in grave danger for the rest of our lives.

I'll Do it MY Way

The Islamists were the Bad Guys for America.

The problem was that now, after all that had happened with the FBI, for me personally, the Good Guys were also "bad guys." I was really convinced that I would be hung out to dry, perhaps successfully revealed to the Sheik's followers as an informant so they would do the dirty work and eliminate me. If that failed, I could be portrayed as a spy, or worse, as a terrorist.

And so I decided to protect myself and collect evidence of my loyalty by wearing a wire to every meeting. *Every meeting.* With FBI agents and the bad guys. No one ever found about my taping the FBI agents until I revealed it to Andrew McCarthy. Those tapes, my personal tapes, were my only insurance policy and proof of my loyalty.

Sacrificing Us All

If I came back in to begin gathering information again, I knew I would have to wear a wire. And I knew I would have to testify. If I testified at trial, my whole family and I would have to live in witness protection forever. I would give up my American dream that had led me from Kindergarten to these very crossroads. I would give up the very thing that motivated me to give it up. How ironic.

It was not an easy choice. And yet, I had no other.

I knew from recent experience that I couldn't live with the guilt of more deaths on my conscience when these guys struck again. The cell was still operational and the worst of the leaders were still on the streets. This was a choice I made for all of us. My kids and Karin really didn't have much say in the decision, though the sacrifice would be theirs as well.

Part of my new deal was that I would be warned, before the final bust, in time to bring my sister's family from Egypt to the US to live under protection as well. The Assistant U.S. Attorney involved at the time, agreed to this condition.

But they didn't know about the condition I made with myself: I would do this MY way this time. The first time, I played along. I did what the FBI asked. I gathered the information. I played by the book that law enforcement, on all levels, has to play by. It was complicated, dangerous, often illogical, and, in the 1993 WTC bombing, completely ineffective. Book or no book, this time there were lives to save, and I intended to save them – my own included.

CHAPTER FOURTEEN
In and Wired

I began to frequently visit the mosque again and meet with the fanatics. I returned on the pretext that I was angry about the arrests, declaring I believed the arrests were because they were Muslims. I ranted and raved about the Feds. My anger was real, but I purposely misled the Fanatics as to its root, however I couldn't tell the regular American Muslim people, who have no agenda; what my real role was in tracking and infiltrating the fanatics who wanted mayhem.

Interviews

In the aftermath of the World Trade Center bombs, I did several interviews for reporters, one being Alison Mitchell of the <u>New York Times</u>.

*Emad S. with Alison Mitchell
in NY Times Interview*

*Emad S. with Kevin McCoy in
Newsweek Magazine Interview*

Another was with Kevin McCoy of <u>Newsweek and one more
with Karim Hagi from New York One News</u>. In these interviews, I praised the Sheik, calling him a scholar and a man of
peace. These interviews were part of my plan to get back into
the cell and go even deeper, to get very close to the Sheik and
stop his reign of terror in my America and around the world.
I gave myself the public persona of being his loyal follower.

These interviews would cause me some trouble later
during the Day of Terror trial. However, I didn't realize that
at the time. And in the end, it wouldn't have mattered. Publicly defending the Sheik was necessary to get back into the
cell after the bombing, and I was undercover not under oath.

Loose Web

Once I was back into the mosque and the fringes of the
cell, about March or April 1993, things began to move fast.

I wanted to find out what else these guys might be up to, especially the people under ground I was told about by Saddiq. One bomb exploding successfully didn't mean another would not go off as well.

There were different kinds of men at the mosque. Each had his own ideas, plans, and motives. They were a cross section of the terrorist world as it exists today. Some were driven by religious zeal, others by greed, others by a lust for power. Some were uneducated men with illusions of their own grandeur. Some were anchorless souls looking for a place to belong. Some were just plain crazy. Most were paranoid. All were dangerous.

They might help each other out with materials and contacts and even money, all in the name of jihad, but they were careful about not naming names or giving away more details to each other than necessary. This protected the various operations if one of them were caught; He would not be able to tell what he did not know. Less noble and well thought-out but equally true, this practice kept one Islamist from high-jacking and taking credit for the operation of another; the paranoia was focused inward as well. This secrecy made it difficult for me to get what I needed on tape, it wasn't easy to bind by the rules and laws of the American Justice System and asking open ended questions to let the microphone record the answers for my future juries in the court of law.

There was that fine line again of trying to get statements without entrapping.

The Blind Sheik, as the Amir or Prince of Jihad, kept himself out of most of the details. He incited, instigated, and ordered, but always in veiled language. He would give the idea or suggest the target, but he did not contact the bomb builders or set up times or means, usually. It was hard to pin him to any particular crime. Legally connecting him to a crime was one of my main objectives.

Close Call

I had a phone installed on which I talked to the bad guys. No one else was ever supposed to answer it. It was the only number on which the Blind Sheik followers' called me.

One day, while I was out debriefing with John and Louie, the phone rang. Distracted by whatever she was doing, Karin absentmindedly answered the phone. Bro. Rahman was calling. "May I speak to Brother Emad?"

"Oh, he's not here."

"Where is he?"

"Oh, he went out with his friends from the FBI."

"What?...Oh...OK." He said he would come over and wait for me.

I happened to call to check in with Karin just after this. She said, "Oh, by the way, Bro. Rahman called."

"Brother Rahman?!" Panic! "What? Where? How?" The questions tumbled out!

"Oh, I'm sorry. I picked up the other phone by mistake." Karin's calmness told me she wasn't anywhere near aware of the danger I ran.

"Oh my God! What did you tell him?"

"No, nothing! It's OK. I told him you were out with your FBI friends. He's waiting for you downstairs in the lobby."

"Oh my God! You're gonna get me killed!?" I hung up and immediately explained to John and Louie about Karin and the call. "Guys, Bro. Rahman is in the lobby now waiting for my return, knowing I am out with my friends from the FBI!"

"Oh shit! She's gonna get you killed! So what do you think we should do?"

I thought a minute and came up with a plan.

"You guys go around back and come up the freight elevator. I'll call Karin to let you in. Then hide in the bedroom closet.

"Here, take these ear buds. They're connected to a transmitter on me. You can listen from the bedroom to whatever goes on in the front room, I was always prepared.

"I'll bring Bro. Rahman up the front way, and you can listen to whatever happens. I'll give you a code word." If I said the code word, they'd know a gun was being pulled. They'd come out firing and try to get him before he got me. I knew

125

Bro. Rahman had an arsenal of weapons. I'd seen them. In fact, the FBI even drained a lake near his house looking for them later, but they were gone.

And so that's what we did. I walked into the lobby where the brother was waiting. "Hey, Bro. Rahman, how are you?"

"Where have you been, Emad?"

"Can you believe this? These FBI agents sonovabitches want me to spy on you guys and the brothers in the mosque. They came around wanting to recruit me." I started to curse and call them names. And I took Brother Rahman straight upstairs to our fifth floor apartment. I glanced at Karin, and she assured me with an eye signal that the agents were in place. We went into the front room to sit and talk.

"Tell me about the FBI," Bro. Rahman said.

I said they had knocked at the door before, but I declined to go out. This time they said they just wanted to talk to me. So I thought I'd go see what they wanted. "They wanted to recruit me! Can you believe it?" I went on awhile, making up this and that.

He said, "OK." He pretended to be convinced and eventually left. John and Louie came out.

"What do you think will happen?" they asked, worried, with good reason.

"I don't know. I think I have to be careful. But he doesn't seem too upset or anything. I think he believes the story." Everybody went home, but the worst was yet to come.

Repercussions

That week Bro. Rahman talked to Dr. Rashid.

Clement Rodney Hampton-El was a Black Muslim it was believed that he was involved in Mostafa Shalaby's murder. A distrustful man, he was commonly known as "Doctor Rashid."

Dr. Rashid especially trusted no one. He decided they had to check out this guy, this retired Egyptian who appeared out of nowhere, and frisk him. But they were thinking, if he does work with the FBI and is wired, we have to be careful not to get caught.

On Sunday, Bro. Rahman called and said, "Dr. Rashid and I want to go for a ride. Come with us." I understood that Karin's answering the phone and talking about the FBI had brought this on, so I had to say ok. However, I took my precautions. I wired myself in a different way.

They drove me to Brooklyn, and there they opened the front gate of an elementary school, deserted on Sunday, of course. We walked into a classroom deep in the school, well secluded from the outside world, well out of hearing distance – of screams or of shots.

And Bro. Rahman started.

"Bro. Emad, you say you are a martial artist. I'm wondering, if someone got a gun and put it in your back - let me show you how," and he grabbed me by the hand. He was making it like a game, like he wanted to know what my martial art experience looked like; but the fact of the matter is, they wanted to know if I was wired or not. He took me to the blackboard and he said, "Ok, if your hand is on the blackboard like that, - spread your legs," and he spread my legs. He got rough and really into the act.

My mind was spinning.

He had me spread against the blackboard. The gun was in his right hand, pressed into my back. Then his left hand came around my body, and he started to frisk my shirt.

Fortunately, I really do have a black belt in martial arts. In the middle of what he was doing, with my right elbow, I swung 'round and blew the gun off my back as quickly as I could. It flew all the way across the floor to the end of the class. It really is a martial arts technique.

I said, "That's what I would do." When I had swung around and hit the gun, I turned face to face with him and pretended that I could punch him, like I was ready to defend myself.

Emad S. Undercover

Dr. Rashid stood up immediately, upset that I blew Rahman's gun away. "No, no, no. It's not that way. Let me show you how." And Rashid took the gun off the floor, came back to me, and put me back spread eagle against the board. With his right hand, he put the gun at the back of my head. With his left, he started to search my chest for the wire.

Immediately, with my right hand, I hit the gun out of his hand again it flew across the room, and I turned around, pretending to be angry. "What the f--- is going on? Are you guys trying to frisk me? Are you crazy?" I yelled right in their faces. I ripped my shirt wide open to show there was nothing on my chest. I kept screaming. Then I turned my back to them and slid my pants down, together with the underwear in one movement (to hide where the wire was hidden) "Will somebody come stick his finger in my butt to see if there's a microphone there? Maybe you will find a microphone in my ass!"

They got embarrassed and said, "Brother, brother, it's ok. Just put your clothes on and let's go." I continued to pretend I was very upset and angry that they mistrusted me and so on. They tried to calm me down. My chest was still uncovered. Seeing my pants down to my knees was quite embarrassing to them.

Can you imagine the stress I felt being with two guys, with a gun, on Sunday in an elementary school with nobody around?

I was not afraid, but I was so stressed, my nerves on high alert. I was in their hands. They could have done anything. How could I get out of that? I think it was only God's grace I was able to pull that off.

I got dressed, still acting angry and offended. They kept apologizing as we got back in the car. It was a long drive home.

CHAPTER FIFTEEN
Bombs Again

Safe house

One of the men closest to the Sheik was Saddiq Ibrahim Saddiq Ali. I made his acquaintance at the mosque and began to gain his trust. He talked often about plans and jihad. He had a lot of big ideas, a lot of targets and operations that he talked about, the Lincoln and the Holland Tunnels, the United Nations building, the Statue of Liberty, and the World Trade Center again to tell the Americans that we can get them anytime we want. But much of what he said was in an odd, inconsistent code, like "big house" for the UN building and "the hadota" instead of bomb. I had to get something concrete for the tapes.

Emad S. during Surveillance of a target

One day Saddiq gave me $300 in cash and asked me to rent a safe house.

Saddiq's cash

Where he could start building bombs. Quickly understanding the value of what was happening, I took the cash carefully and placed it in a plastic bag, taking care not to smudge Saddiq's fingerprints.

I took the request to John and Louie, along with the money in the bag. The FBI got Saddiq's fingerprints off the bills. This exchange of funds was the action that verified Saddiq's intentions to blow up NY targets. Now we had a case.

It was decided the JTTF would rent and wire a place for the bomb making to happen under their direct control.

One morning, John and Louie picked me up and drove me to the Federal Plaza, where I was introduced to a new supervisor, Ron Muhafi, who the JTTF had decided would be the coordinator facilitating the safe house. He was a former Navy Officer. My experience with "former" anything, other than street humps, had not been very confidence inspiring so far. Being a Navy officer didn't seem to automatically translate into being qualified to work on a terrorist task force in my opinion.

I was proven correct by what happened once we went to the warehouse, which will serve as a bomb factory.

Muhafi drove me in his car from the basement of the Federal Plaza into Jamaica in Queens. I noticed that we were followed by three cars with more agents, to secure the process of me receiving the keys to the safe-house, now equipped with state-of-the-art audio and video surveillance. Ron parked our car at a warehouse across the street. Then he grabbed his radio to instruct the other agents to "lay low" and not attract attention.

I was shocked.

Every passer-by on the sidewalk was staring at him, talking on his radio, telling the rest of the humps not to draw attention! Okay....

But who the heck I was, telling him to do otherwise?

After Mr. Muhafi got acknowledgements from the rest of the humps that they understood his instructions, he opened his driver- side door and started crossing the street on foot toward the warehouse... but he had no jacket on to hide his exposed gun and badge on his belt. Like THAT wouldn't attract attention!

Of course I had to follow him to the safe house, which is no longer safe in my opinion, but I couldn't hold my big, fat mouth from blasting him in front of his agents.

"This is crazy! What are you doing?"

The bomb factory in Queens (NY Post)

"What?"

"Did you see how you crossed the street with your gun on your belt? Is that how you lay low?"

Only then did he realize what he was doing. Embarrassed in front of his agents, Ron said, "It's okay!"

"Not okay! Everybody in the neighborhood was staring at you when you were talking on your radio to your agents, and then, you crossed the street displaying your gun. This is crazy! I am not going to do my work in this place. The whole neighborhood now knows that something is going on in here."

"No, no - it's okay!"

"It is NOT okay! Only my ass will be on the line, working here!" Some of the other agents tried to convince me that it was going to be alright. I had my doubts.

Muhafi had met with the technicians who installed the cameras and microphones, and he asked them to point out the surveillance equipment locations to me. I was not happy about the microphones' locations, since the distance between some of the microphones was 50 feet, enough to create a big echo in the sound being recorded. But… who the hell is this Emad Salem to tell them differently.

Then I asked for a table to be put in one of the corners of the room for putting together my electronics. I made sure it was in a corner where they said the cameras and microphones were pointing to.

I received the keys, and we headed back to the Federal Plaza. There was complete silence in the car and up to the meeting room on the 28th floor of the Federal Building, but then a shouting match ensued between Ron Muhafi and me. He insisted on defending his actions, and I was just being a "pain in the ass. "

I was right, though, about coming from the Navy not being enough to give Mr. Muhafi the experience and knowledge to work covertly.

As I anticipated, when it came to the translation of the audio retrieved from the warehouse, we had to listen to every word 5 times because of the echo in the sound. Altogether, it took 2 years to finish.

On the other hand, I will never forget the Egyptian translator Gamal Abdel Hafez. He was very intelligent, methodical and helpful in the translations because he was an Al Azhar University graduate and has great command of the Arabic language. His ambition and his great love of America, which we share, helped him to become a Special Agent in the FBI later on. Also, I wouldn't want to forget Frank Nalu, the Iraqi FBI linguistic, and his valuable help with the translations over those two years.

Frank Nalu (FBI Linguistic)

Unsafe Safe house

Now I had the keys for the safe house in Jamaica, Queens to use as a bomb-building factory. The Feds wired it for audio and video before I took Saddiq there.

Saddiq asked me to build a small model or experimental bomb. I got some M80's, and put together what appeared to be a model bomb. We drove out into Connecticut and set off the device in a deserted area, I made sure that my recording devices were in operating mode to capture the sound of the explosion. It was enough, apparently, to satisfy Saddiq that I did know what I was doing.

Having shown that I could, indeed, handle explosives, Saddiq began to make more definite plans for bigger and better operations.

CHAPTER SIXTEEN
Getting Close to the Sheik

Saddiq asked if, in my capacity as a surveillance expert, I could run a sweep of the Blind Sheik's apartment, upon the Sheik's request. Omar Abdel Rahman was nervous, after the arrests from the 1993 WTC bombing, that he was being spied upon by the Feds. "I don't know if the FBI is monitoring my apartment." Omar Abdel Rahman said.

Emad S. with the Blind Sheik

This was my perfect opportunity. I wanted to catch the Sheik speaking on tape if he makes incriminating statements that would serve to arrest and convict him of the crimes he is always planning and instigating.

Control Freak

I went to John Anticev and asked him for a sweeping device. He went to Carson Dunbar and requested one for me. Dunbar sent them to Radio Shack. I remember that day. It was John Anticev and Louie Napoli in a black limo. Also along was an FBI bomb expert, Steve Vierra.

They found a store with a suitable device, so they called Carson. They gave him the price. "It's $300."

He said, "It's too expensive, keep looking for a cheaper device." It blows my mind to see three federal agents driving around Manhattan in a limousine for five hours to save maybe fifty dollars.

They got back in the car and drove some more. Stop. Call. "No, too expensive." Back in the car and off to another store. Same thing: too expensive, no authorization. Such control. Why not authorize a price and let them do their job? He didn't trust his agents to spend even three hundred dollars, to fight a known terrorist, without his stamp of approval. Did he not trust anybody?

I finally got sick of the charade. I was going to fight this terrorist cell and catch these guys before any more bombings happen again, there was my resolve to do it my way this time, not Carson Dunbar's. He seemed to get cold feet right at pivotal moments…moments that too often left me hanging out to dry.

Not this time. I finally said, "You know what? The clock is ticking. The Sheik expects me to have this by 6 O'clock. So I'm going to buy one." From my P.I. days, I knew where to buy what I needed, and I bought it. Out of pocket. Three hundred dollars. Forget the Suits.

I was so mad that three Federal agents were getting paid who-knows-how-much per hour, driving around Manhattan for five hours just to save $50. It's crazy. The only explanation was Dunbar's reluctance to trust his own guys to make simple decisions – or else he just didn't want me to have equipment bought with Fed money.

I needed the device that day because I had to sweep the Sheik's apartment right away. But Carson was so adamant about not giving me access to Federal equipment – because he thought I wasn't trustworthy. Once again he put me in danger of being found out.

Clean Sweep – Sort Of

I was already somewhat familiar with the apartment. My strategy was to convince the Sheik that the entire apartment was bugged except for the kitchen. I chose the kitchen because it was the smallest, most confined space in the apartment. The cupboards were wooden and will not reflect sound. I knew that if I took my wired briefcase to record him in the bigger rooms, the sound would echo. Another advantage of using the kitchen was that it was too small for more than two or three of us at a time. No audiences as I talked to the Sheik and tried to capture his voice.

Emad S. preparing recording device

The kitchen was perfect.

As I swept the apartment, I walked around the rooms with the device in my right hand and the Sheik holding onto my left arm. The correct way to use the device is to lower the volume in a neutral place, and then start to do your sweep. When you come to a spot where there is a transmitter or any kind of electromagnetic field, the machine makes that high-pitched sound. *Eeeeee...*

The Sheik, of course, is blind. He couldn't see my finger on the volume. As we walked up to a wall, I turned up the volume so that he thought it was picking up a signal from an FBI monitoring device. In this way, I convinced him all of the other rooms in his apartment were bugged. But when we went to the kitchen, I turned the volume very low and told him, "I'm not picking up any bugs here."

Our conversations began to take place here in this tiny room.

Now the problem was that if I was taking the Sheik to the kitchen, why would I take my briefcase? With twelve of his followers in the front room...if they found me out, beheading was the punishment. But I just played dumb and went with it. I took chances and I took the Sheik and the briefcase/recording device to the kitchen.

Bayat – Blood Oath

Saddiq had passed along a message that the Sheik wanted me to give him a bayat. A bayat is an oath of allegiance, where you put your very life at the service of the Sheik. It is a solemn vow, and breaking it can cost your life.

I didn't want to be suspected of being less than completely faithful and loyal. So I decided to give a bayat to the Sheik. We were at his apartment, which I had "swept." Since I had led him to believe the kitchen was the only clean spot in the house, the Sheik suggested that we should go to the kitchen where there are no bugs.

I gave a bayat to the Blind Sheik. I swore to put him and his cause and his life ahead of my own. To sacrifice my life for his, if necessary. Or to sacrifice it just because he said I should. That's the nature of jihad.

Swearing a bayat of allegiance to the Blind Sheik was the only way to gain his full confidence and get what I needed. What the FBI needed. What America and the Justice Department needed not to forget that Egypt also needed. In this dramatic event I had to shed some tears, but to convince the Sheik that I was sincere in my bayat to him.

It did not bother me to swear an oath I would not honor to save many more lives than my own, to protect the country I love from an evil man who twists the truth and uses Islam to radicalize young men just to work his own agenda. That is not an ethical problem at all. That is what is right, that was the undercover role I was doing. It is the cost of freedom. Another lesson for American leaders to learn.

Gotcha!

When I recorded one of the key tapes, Central Monitoring #28 (CM28), we were in the kitchen, the small space. I had sworn the bayat, the blood oath. Sheik Omar now felt comfortable to bring me into his inner cell. Even though I had told him there were no bugs in the kitchen, he was still careful. He leaned in to whisper in my ear and to give me orders.

I didn't know what he was going to tell me, but every word had to be recorded, just in case. There was no telling when something important would be said. I needed to get the recording device in the brief case close enough to catch his whispered words. Blind people have sharper hearing and other senses, as they say. I was so afraid he would be able to sense the briefcase as I brought it right up close to his mouth. But if I didn't take this risk, all of my efforts could be for nothing. And I was right.

The tapes picked up his fatwa that bombing the U.N. is not illicit, but he wanted me to go after the Army instead. He said, rightly so, that an attack against the U.N. would look like Muslims were against peace and would turn the world against the Muslim cause. He had other ideas instead.

"Find a way to inflict damage on the American Army…" There. He said it. And I had my tape-loaded briefcase right up to his mouth and my ear when he said it. He was on tape as directly ordering an attack on American military.

That is the tape that put him away. It was what made the conviction. It was Sunday when this conversation took place in the kitchen yet I couldn't wait to call John & Louie to bring them in to the Federal Plaza on Sunday to listen and confirm that the tape captured the Sheik's Fatwa and it did. At this moment only I think that I was able to do what so many other undercover agents in different countries including Egypt could not do, capture Sheik Omar red handed, he is cunning and slick enough not to leave his fingerprints on any of the crimes he instigated. He always had people drop dead yet he got away with it.

Bodyguard

Once I gave a bayat to the Blind Sheik, he trusted me without limit. Very soon, I was his bodyguard, translator and personal servant. I lived in his home and washed his dishes. I put his shoes on his feet. I studied him. I KNEW him.

Emad S. the bodyguard

I knew that some of his followers were less than loyal. When his next-door neighbor (Abdel Rahman Hagag) sent his wife to cook for the Sheik, as he was blind, after all, the Sheik found ways to touch her and rub against her breasts, to the extent that she felt he was inappropriate. This made Abdel Rahman Hagag very angry, and he was not particularly careful about his comments against the Sheik after that.

CHAPTER SEVENTEEN
Intelligent Intelligence Gathering

I wasn't just sitting around making tapes and getting the Sheik coffee. I had some discussions with the Sheik's followers.

We did a lot of talking as well during those days. I came to understand that the targets were major US and NY landmarks: the United Nations building, FBI Headquarters, the Lincoln and Holland Tunnels, Washington bridge, The Statue of Liberty, Grand central station and the Military Armory in Manhattan.

Regarding the assassinations and kidnaping it was Henry Kissinger, Senator D'Amato, Judge Duffy and Dov Hikend the Jewish assemblyman in New York.

Much of what I gathered on tape would be used later in the case against these evildoers and would get them off the streets of my America. This material would form the basis for the case in what they called the "Trial of the Century. "Or "the day of terror trial"

But sometimes I gather other information that could be used immediately to stop someone or stop something from happening.

Foiling Plots

Hosni Mubarak, the president of Egypt, was considered an infidel by the Sheik, as I mentioned. This made him fair game for anybody wanting to put a notch in his jihad belt.

I uncovered a plot to assassinate the Egyptian President Mubarak.

In another instance, I was able to find out the location of Mahmoud Abouhalima, also known as "The Red," for his unusual red beard. He had been in the Afghan wars. Then he came to the US and was one of the participants in the WTC bombing in 1993. He was also suspected in the murder of Mostafa Shalaby, the mosque leader who refused to give Sheik Omar the million dollars the mosque had collected for jihad in Afghanistan. Clutched in Mostafa Shalaby's dead hand were red hairs, and Abouhalima was known to hang around with those suspected of the murder.

The Red fled the country after the WTC bombing and went to Saudi Arabia to perform his Omra (a Muslim ceremony to visit El Kaaba) then he went back to Egypt to his mother's house where he was arrested by the Egyptian Feds and it didn't take very long for him to admit to the Egyptian Feds the Blind Sheik's involvement in issuing a fatwa to bomb the World Trade Center and he started to spill the beans.

Sometimes, swift action was required. Going by the book or going through channels cost time and met with road blocks or got lost in the shuffle of papers and memos that flew around federal offices and between bureaucrats. In the case of the assassination attempt on Hosni Mubarak, if I had not gone straight to the Egyptians, the bombing would have been history before the information got passed along. Fortunately, I did pass it along and saved lives. But in doing so, I made people angry. Very angry for violating the so called protocol so I should report to my handler, who will write a memo and put on his supervisor's desk who will read it and write another memo to the assistant special agent in charge who will read it and write another memo to his headquarters, and God only knows how long before action will be taken.

Trouble with Egypt

My work for the FBI violated my retirement conditions in Egypt. As a retired high-ranking military officer in the Egyptian army, I cannot work for another foreign intelligence agency without presidential approval. My work with the FBI was in violation of that law. I became the subject of an

Egyptian military tribunal, with a possible prison sentence in Egypt.[3]

President Hosni Mubarak was considered an enemy of the Muslim Brotherhood because he did not sufficiently promote the idea of an Islamic state in Egypt. The Sheik told me I had sinned in working for an infidel. I could atone for that and prove my loyalty by shooting President Mubarak in an upcoming visit to New York. I played along, but I called friends in Egypt who were able to get the trip cancelled.

At a later point, Saddiq Ali was talking one day of a plan to send two MIG 17s from Sudan to drop missiles on the Presidential Palace. "Essam Gilgale is a Sudanese military pilot waiting for the green light," Saddiq told me. The MIGs would then turn and crash into the U.S. Embassy in Cairo, in Tahrir Square. The two pilots would eject themselves before the crash, Saddiq asked me as a former Egyptian Commander if I can pretend that I am arresting the pilots in Tahrir Square, then I should drive them into a safe haven (The Su-

---

3   One condition of my Egyptian retirement was that I could not do intelligence work for any foreign country. Clearly, my work for American FBI violated this condition. One day, I was talking on the phone to a friend in Egyptian Intel, a Brigadier. He was telling me about this tribunal for which I was wanted because of this violation. I reminded him that I saved the US Embassy and I saved Mubarak's life. "Won't that work in my favor?"

"Well, I'll see what I can do." He sent some memos to the Defense Minister and all the way up to the Presidential Palace, and I got a pardon. All the charges were dropped. My Brigadier friend gave me the green light. I was free to visit Egypt.

danese Embassy in Cairo) I pretended that it was easy to do so and it was a piece of cake. But to tell you the truth I was horrified that Saddiq might have some other former military officers like Ali Mohamed who used to train Osama Bin Ladin's Bodyguards and was an informant for the FBI and the CIA and he was an active sergeant in the American Green Beret.

Saddiq Ali the cell leader

This was the first time they talked about using airplanes as missiles. I was fortunate to have this on tape. I went straight home and called Egyptian intelligence.

"Hey Guys, raise up your awareness towards the Black Country. Two birds might sneak in and download at the boss's house and then turn on the U.S. Embassy."

"How positive is it?"

"It's positive."

"Thank you."

Egypt immediately upped its radar air defenses toward Sudan and closed the window of opportunity for the attack.

I made the call to Egypt from my home phone. That phone was being tapped by the FBI; I knew this. At the time, I was helping build bombs. It was a good precaution the FBI was taking. But I didn't worry about making the call. I wasn't doing anything wrong. I was protecting the American Embassy and the President of Egypt.

I got hell the next day.

"How dare you call Egyptian Intelligence!?" John Anticev yelled. He was furious. "I would have handled it. You should have just passed that along to us."

"Handle it? You're going to write a memo to your supervisor; and your supervisor will write a memo to your ASAC; and your ASAC will write a memo to Washington; and Washington will write a memo to the State Department; and the State Department would write -- . The guy would already be killed. The Embassy would be bombed!"

It was stupid. Most likely, his superior was on him about it, about not having his asset under control.

Yemen

To make this point even clearer, I will relate something that happened after I was in witness protection. It reinforces this issue, so I'll tell it here.

In 2000, Egyptian Feds managed to get a message to me. They wanted me to come to Egypt. I called Louie Napoli and told him about it.

"Why do they need you?" he asked

"I don't know."

"Are you Ok with that?"

"I am not." I wasn't feeling very good about it. But after we talked a while, I decided I would go and see what was up. I did tell Louie, "If I don't call you in forty-eight hours after I get there, I need you to raise hell with the American Embassy."

I did call Louie after I arrived to let him know I was ok. Though I wasn't very comfortable with this whole thing, I met with Egyptian Feds. "You have done a good job with the Americans. Now we need you to do something for us. We need to send you to a country with lots of mountains."

"Ok. Yemen." I was tired of guessing games. "Keep going…"

I was taken to another meeting with very high-ranking federal officials. "We need you to go into Yemen as a covert agent. We're going to have somebody there to assist you, and then you take it from there. Something is being cooked up right now, and we don't know what it is. Can you get in?"

"That's what I do." I said

"Ok. Go get in. What do you need?"

"I need pictures, names, backgrounds. And I need something else."

The Lt. Colonel speaking said, "Don't f***ing tell me money…"

"I don't need your money. Keep your money. But I need the green light from the American Feds."

"Are you nuts!? Americans should not know about this at all."

"You're crazy. You want me to go into Yemen to operate covertly? I'm an American citizen, and you want me to go under? If I'm captured or blown, who's going to get me out?"

"Don't worry. Americans can't know."

"Well that's a deal breaker. I'm willing to do it. If there's something being cooked, and you don't know what it is, I'm going to tell you what it is. I'm going to go in and bring you the details. But if any CIA agent sees me who knows my face, they'll go report that I'm working for a foreign country." I am an American citizen.

"Foreign!? We became 'foreign' now?" the Lt. Colonel shouted.

"No. You're not foreign. Egypt is my mother country, and I owe you everything. When I was a baby with my bottle, I was sucking Egyptian milk. Don't tell me I'm not loyal.

"But I became an American citizen. I have to get the green light from the American Feds. If something was being cooked against the U.S., they would welcome my finding out. It's a common interest," I told them.

"No, no, no! This should NOT be revealed to them!"

"Then the deal's off. I won't do it."

I had helped to clean up the Egyptian streets from Sheik Omar and some of his followers while I was in the United States, so don't tell me I have no loyalty to Egypt.

I came home from my trip. Louie met with me. "Louie, they wanted me to go to Yemen."

"Yemen? You're an old man. What are you going to do in the caves there? What do they want in Yemen?"

I answered, "I don't know. Something is cooking, and they want me to go in covertly and find out. They didn't want to give me the green light to share the operation with the American FBI."

"OK, then forget about it. It's ok. You're back. You're safe now." So I forgot about it - until a few months later, when it all made sense.

I was sitting watching TV, and boom! There it was! The USS Cole had just been bombed. "Honey," I yelled to my wife, "remember Yemen? They just bombed the USS Cole!"

I don't know if Louie ever passed that information up the pipeline. I don't know if he even should have. It was all very unofficial. The FBI has to work by the book and do the right thing so their cases will stand up, even if it gets in the way of the work they are supposed to be doing.

If Egypt had been willing to share information with the US, I could have gone to Yemen. Who knows what the result could have been?

Sadly 17 American sailors were killed in that bombing and hundreds of thousands of dollars worth of damage to the American destroyer USS Cole.

Kidnapping John Anticev

Back to 1993. One evening, I received a phone call from Ahmed Abdel Sattar. "Brother Emad, we have to do the evening prayer in the Abou Bakr Mosque in Queens."

I said, "Of course, Brother Ahmed. Of course." I got the message that something important would take place at the Abou Bakr Mosque that night.

Sattar and Sheik Omar Abdel Al Rahman

Ahmed Abdel Sattar worked in the U.S. Postal Service. He had revealed to me in a previous conversation that he would go to the mailroom and get the area codes of US military units overseas and decode them to know their exact locations. He then sent this information to the Brothers in Egypt, so they could arrange attacks on our military overseas.

After the evening prayer, Ahmed Abdel Sattar and Ali Shinawy went to the basement of the Abou Bakr Mosque to discuss an "important issue." To my surprise, it was a plan to kidnap Special Agent John Anticev as a bargain to release El Sayyid Nosair from prison in exchange with Agent John.

Ahmed Abdel Sattar, through his work in the Postal Service, was able to obtain John Anticev's home address. They knew right where he lived.

It was almost midnight by now, and I had run out of recording tapes. This was a major event, which had to be documented; I had to have it on tape kidnapping my John was like an attack on me personally that was my agent and case handler and I liked him enough to call him sometimes a friend. So I excused myself, ran to the pay phone and called John to give him the heads-up and to request more tapes. Unfortunately John didn't answer. I called Louie Napoli instead.

As usual, Louie's answer was, "I am on my way!" I went back to the basement to continue our conversation and act natural until I received a page that Louie had arrived in a dark alley around the back of the mosque. I slipped out to meet him. I was shocked to see a woman in the driver's seat and Louie in the passenger's seat. Louie's wife was driving! She had to be part of the action! In reality, her shining the headlights of her car allowed Louie and me to stick our heads into the trunk of my car as we loaded the new tape.

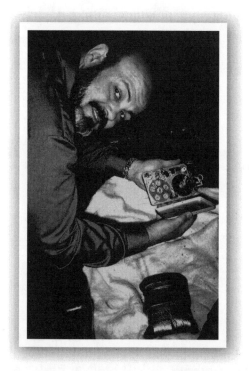

Emad S. preparing the recording device

I ran back to tape what was left of the kidnapping plot.

The next morning at 6:00 a.m., John Anticev started out for his daily jog, knowing nothing of the night's activities.

To his surprise, he met Ahmed Abdel Sattar right near his house. John asked, "What are you doing here?"

Sattar's answer was not satisfactory to John's investigative mind. John was uncomfortable with Sattar's presence so near his home that early in the morning.

John was even more alarmed after I met with him at 8:00 a.m. to be debriefed. He was shocked to hear from me that we had been discussing his kidnapping just the night before, so we could bargain with the FBI to exchange John for El Sayyid Nosair, Meir Kahana's assassin. Nosair was serving time in Attica prison.

John wanted to know who was at the meeting. I said Sattar and Shinawy. John said, "Can you believe it? I met Sattar outside my house this morning!" It was not a surprise to me.

John informed the Bureau, and they provided extra security details around his house.

Cross-Sharing

Information sharing is tricky, too. Carson Dunbar didn't like Nancy Floyd, of another department – the Russian Squad, to have any knowledge of the information I gathered for the JTTF and the FBI. There is no trust and little willingness to cooperate between departments. This has something to do with some regulations laid down to protect officers and assets, but common sense must over-ride such considerations for intelligence to be effective, in my opinion.

There is even less trust between nations, even close allies.

CHAPTER EIGHTEEN
Disposable

Leak

Soon after I started putting together materials for us to create actual bombs, Carson Dunbar wanted to close the operation and arrest Saddiq. We had him on tape talking about bombing the U.N., and we had his fingerprints on the money he gave me to rent a bomb-making facility. When he gave me actual money and specific instruction, he showed by action, not only intent, that he was really serious in carrying out the bombings he had just talked about this time. Saddiq was in the bag. Carson seemed content to settle for this one terrorist. He was a former state trooper, not an FBI hump-turned-suit. He was not ready to do what it takes to put an operation like this in place, the hours and effort and danger that had brought us this far. He was willing to spend it all for one arrest, and not the biggest fish at that.

Whatever his reasons, those of us working the case were not in agreement and pushed to keep it alive. But Carson had his "defendant."

I think that he didn't need or want me anymore. What better way to get rid of an irritating asset than to have him found out by the bad guys and murdered. Not very original, but clever, nonetheless. Very convenient and very clean.

Coincidentally – or not, immediately after this disagreement, The New York Post released that there was new terror cell targeting New York.

The NY Post leak

Disposable

It saddens me to see how eager I was to catch the "bad guys" after the 1993 WTC bombing but having to fight one of the Suits at that time to be able to continue the undercover work to bring out the underground people who are still lurking in American Streets.

I was told by one of the ASAC later on: "Be careful. You are disposable, when it comes to the FBI."

I thought that I was doing a good job as an American Citizen. I thought that, as a good citizen trying to help, I would have to fear nothing but the bad guys who wanted to hurt my America.

Little did I know that the reason I had to cover my ass from one of the Suits was not because I was doing something wrong, but because I think that they wanted to cover up their personal vindictiveness against me. There was no plan B or any intention to round up the rest of the cell.

I did not know an American Citizen could be "disposable" simply because he comes from a different Background. I am an American citizen as much as the President, despite the fact that I was not born here. Individuals who were trying to cover up their mistakes or lack of ethics will not shake my love for "my America".

It was incomprehensible to see The New York Post article revealing my undercover operation. At the same time I was adamant about preventing the next bombing attack, there were others who were trying desperately to cover up their mistakes, even if the price was my life. I had operated undercover for a whole entire month after the front-page article which blew my cover.

I don't think any of these agents would have continued the undercover work, putting their lives at risk, after reading that article in The New York Post. But I don't think I was stupid either, in continuing the work, because I know that many, many Americans would have been killed if I hadn't. Federal Prosecutor Andrew McCarthy agreed with this position in his book, *Willful Blindness*. And Judge Michael Mukasey, who tried the case, said, "This plot could have produced devastation on a scale unknown to this country since the Civil War."[4]

I wonder why none of the Suits or Humps raised up their voices to request an investigation in order to come to the bottom of this. Why didn't they try to find the person who leaked secret, covert undercover operations to the newspaper, putting my life in danger? Everyone knows you don't talk about an operation while an informant is building five bombs, which would have devastated New-York City. I hope the answer is not because I am disposable.

---

4   http://www.nytimes.com/2007/09/20/washington/20trial.html?page-wanted=all&_r=2&

Post was 1st to reveal second terrorist cell

If you think you've already heard about a "second cell" of terrorists in New York, you're right.

Word of another group of terrorists connected to the World Trade Center bombers was first revealed in an exclusive New York Post story a month ago.

In a Page One headline on May 25, The Post, announced: "New Terror Cell Targets N.Y. Pol / Twin Tower probe reveals 2nd threat."

We reported FBI agents had notified police that a second cell of Arab terrorists had targeted Brooklyn Assemblyman Dov Hikind for assassination.

The story revealed the FBI had learned of the planned assassination on May 17, when it intercepted information from cell members.

The FBI and police refused to comment just how the information was intercepted, and clamped a tight

NEW YORK POST

NEW TERROR CELL TARGETS N.Y. POL

Twin Tower probe reveals 2d threat

FLASHBACK: How The Post broke the story.

lid of secrecy on their investigation.

But the lid came off yesterday. In an official complaint filed in federal court, it was revealed the information came from a confidential FBI informant inside the second cell.

Based on the information, Hikind has been under round-the-clock police protection since May 17.

The NY Post bragging about the leak

Everybody chose to turn a blind eye or play deaf to this unethical crime, a crime I think happened in order to cover the person who leaked it. Is that ethical behavior? I think if Mr. Louis Frey, the Director of the FBI at that time, had known that his New York office had leaked this information, he would have taken action. You ask me why I think so? I will tell you: it is because he was a Hump before he became the biggest Suit.

I am pointing to and emphasizing this incident in the hope that it will not happen again in the future. It MUST NOT happen again, if we want the Muslim Community's cooperation in the War on Terrorism. And we need its cooperation in order to win this war on terrorism.

Being disposable for the FBI, to cover someone's mistakes, is not the same as being disposable for America. Clearly, the people who did not die in the averted bombings would not think I am disposable, if they knew that they wouldn't be here now, working and raising their families, if not for my work. Thankfully, they do not even know the disaster they missed. I was not disposable for America.

And I am not disposable to my wife and kids, to my whole family.

Since my case came to its successful end, we have been exposed to many different terrorist attacks. I remember Richard Reid (the Shoe Bomber), Omar Farouk Abdulmutallab (the Nigerian Underwear Bomber) and Faisal Shahzad (the Times Square Bomber.) I am almost sure that there was somebody who knew something about these attacks beforehand, but they did not come forward. It was only God's grace and protection of my America, that these attacks were foiled.

Richard Reid's bomb shoe

Abdel Motaleb the underwear bomber

Faisal Shahzad the Time Square bomber

If the FBI wants the cooperation of the Muslim community to prevent future terrorist attacks, they have to realize that they cannot treat Middle Easterners and other Muslims as disposable citizens.

Pressing On

My handlers and I were shocked and concerned. My handlers wanted to go ahead and pull me out, take me to a safe house. I was not convinced my cover had been blown. There hadn't been any change in attitude toward me at the mosque. Saddiq was business-as-usual. I really wanted to get the Sheik on tape to disclose his knifing instigations and provocations through his fatwas, and I thought I could still do it.

I went back to the mosque. It seemed only a little risky. But back then, not yet knowing the end of the story made for a lot of uncertainty. We all knew if I were caught, there would be torture and abuse before a grisly beheading death. But we were so close…and nothing seemed to have changed. I felt sure I could convince the terrorists I was still one of them.

I have been accused of being arrogant or wanting to be a hero. It isn't arrogant to know your own abilities. You understand your foes, and you do a good evaluation of the possibility of success. That is confidence. We need more confidence in actual abilities today.

And, there's nothing wrong with wanting to be a hero. Hero is not a dirty word. We need more heroes.

CHAPTER NINETEEN
Bombs Away!

Sudan

Saddiq was from Sudan, and Sudan came up often in my dealings with these terrorists.

Sudan's involvement began long ago, even before the Sheik ran jihad operations from there, between his escape from house arrest in Egypt and his procuring a visa for the US from our embassy in Sudan. Sudan's links with terrorism were clear and obvious. And yet, we accepted a Sudanese ambassador on American soil.

Several of the terrorists in New York hailed from Sudan.

One night Saddiq and I sat all night in his New Jersey apartment, talking about the operations and bombings he wanted to accomplish. Around 4:00 a.m., he started talking about bombing what he called "the Big House" – the United Nations Building. Curious now, and wanting to see what I could get on tape, I asked if he already had a fatwa from the Sheik for this operation.

"No, I do not have the fatwa yet, but I have a facilitator who will assist us to carry out the Big House operation."

"Really?"

"Yes. The Sudanese ambassador."

Honestly, I did not believe him. This sounded like very big talk. But at 6:00 in the morning, he picked up the phone and dialed a number. To my surprise, someone answered and arranged to meet with us at ten o'clock at the Sudanese Embassy. I could not believe that Saddiq was powerful enough to call the Sudanese ambassador at his home at six in the morning.

I knew I had to inform John & Louie about this.

I excused myself to go home and shower and change clothes and get extra recording equipment.

John Anticev and Louie Napoli responded to my call and arrived at my apartment at 7:30 that morning. As usual, John gave me extra tapes, but Louie warned me about carrying a recording device into the Sudanese Mission (or Embassy). It is considered Sudanese sovereign territory. I would have to go through inspection upon entry. If I got caught inside the Sudanese Ambassador's office, the FBI would have no jurisdiction to help me get out. I understood, and told him ok.

However, I couldn't resist the opportunity to document this meeting on tape. I took my briefcase with three hours of tape and went with Saddiq to the Embassy.

I was concerned that the magnetometer at the checkpoint would ruin my tapes before the meeting could even take place. I made sure to open it for a physical inspection instead. Luckily, it passed without raising any suspicion.

To my surprise, Saddiq was very casual in his conversation with the embassy diplomat. The Sudanese official promised to provide us with a Diplomatic license plate to put on a stolen limousine to carry the bomb into the United Nations building.

Then Saddiq came up with a new request for the diplomat– the itinerary of Boutros Boutros- Ghali, president of the UN at the time.

Boutros Ghali

The request was met with a big grin from the diplomat. He knew Saddiq was after Boutros-Ghali, who he considered a "dirty Coptic," and promised to provide the itinerary.

I thanked God I was able to walk safely out of the embassy with a very incriminating tape that revealed the true face of the Sudanese government. It was not surprising that Louie Napoli was furious when he saw me exit the UN building with that briefcase in hand!

Later, the US State Department finally expelled Ahmed Yousef and Siraj El-Din as having abused their diplomatic privileges at the Sudanese Embassy. Sudan was put on the list of countries supporting terrorism. I really think this recording played a major role in that decision.

Oil Makes the World go Round

We would use ammonium nitrate and diesel oil, mixed in fifty-five gallon drums, five of them, one for each target.

A Palestinian man who owned a gas station in Yonkers would arrange the diesel oil. The station was a money-laundering front to funnel money to Gaza and the West Bank for Hamas, so the owner was called "The Money Man." However, it also came in handy for diesel oils. Mohamed Saleh, agreed to help with the jihad operation by providing the diesel oils for five barrels fifty five gallons each.

Saddiq and I drove to Yonkers and met with Saleh in a park. We sat on the ground and ate lunch. There is a certain protocol or etiquette to be followed, even when the subject is jihad.

Saddiq opened the conversation. "We are starting to do jihad in the US, Brother. Brother Emad, here, is ex-Army and will put the devices together for us."

"Ok, ok, just don't talk out loud about the details."

"Oh, yes, yes, okay," Saddiq answered. Ok, we're going to do the following."

He got a piece of paper and wrote down, "Bomb the United Nations." He showed the paper to Saleh, who said, "Ok, ok."

Saddiq then said, "This paper has to disappear. Bro. Emad, chew this up and swallow it."

While this sounds strange, I had seen this done before by people who needed to make a paper disappear for good. So I took the paper, chewed it up and swallowed it. I took the paper and crushed in a way to make noise and then I put it in my mouth and I started to chew it to get the sounds on tape. Out loud, I said, "OK, I swallowed it! It has vanished in my stomach now."(Later, in court, though I couldn't prove what was written on the paper, the chewing sound and my comments did back up what I testified for.)

By following the instructions of the head of the cell, I was showing my obedience and my dedication to the jihad. It showed Saleh we were tough mujahedin. Again, Saleh said, "Ok, ok. What do you need?"

"We need you to participate in jihad in the US. If you want to plan and carry out something yourself, that's fine. But if not, then you can contribute five drums of diesel oils."

"Ok. You get the fuel. I am busy with the gas station and do not have time to plan anything. Just get me the barrels, and I will give you the diesel oil. That will be my contribution to jihad." That was the end of the discussion that day.

But I was wired and all of it was recorded.

Saddiq sent Amir Abdelgani and his cousin Fadile to Yonkers to pick up the barrels of oil from Mohamed Saleh the next day. Only they didn't go alone: the FBI surveillance team was with them the whole way. They met back with us at the warehouse, where we unloaded the fuel. (See my website for photos of us unloading these barrels from the van to be used for the bombs I should build.)

How Does the Garden Grow?

Fertilizer, of course.

Next Saddiq and I visited a garden center. Saddiq explained to the store clerks that we needed this fertilizer for a big yard we were planting. We loaded five bags of "ammonium nitrate" in my car. I recorded the conversation. The FBI went in the center right after we left and got a copy of the receipt. Back at the safe house in Queens, we unloaded the fertilizer. The FBI had a video of us doing so. The FBI documented the whole thing on film. My website has that video.

Once we had the oil and the fertilizer, Saddiq was ready to go to work. He asked what else we would need.

"Detonators," I told him.

"Ok, we'll go see Dr. Rashid." Before he took me with him, he talked to Dr. Rashid about where to meet. It was agreed we would meet at a safe house in Brooklyn.

All of these developments, of course, were reported to my handlers in our regular debriefing meetings. Louie Napoli told me not to go wired into the Brooklyn safe house. As I said earlier, the group is known for its violence. If I were found to be wired when they frisked me – and they would frisk me, I was dead.

Yet I could not resist the opportunity to get evidence on tape.

Dr. Rashid told me on that day that he and other brothers from his group had held up twelve post offices starting from Atlanta all the way to New York. The money was stolen and used to finance jihad operations and I wanted to document all of his criminal activities on tape. I took my brief case and got by with it. I set it down a little distance from us, so as not to be too conspicuous but also close enough to catch our voices. It was a good thing I did.

Once Rashid started talking and telling stories, he made comments about the Sheik's pronouncement against the money manager of the mosque, Mostafa Shalaby.

Mostafa Shalaby

The reason they chose to rob the post offices was because the infidel government owned them, it was ok, according to the

Sheik's fatwa, to rob these SOB's and take their money for jihad. Dr. Rashid said they had given most of the money to the mosque, as instructed, but they kept back some of it for their own jihad. It was with that cash they had rented the safe house we were sitting in.

The robberies had been at gunpoint. As far as I know, Hampton-El had never been connected with them before this. Until the FBI heard the translations of the tapes, they had no idea who had done the robberies.

During the course of the long conversation, Dr. Rashid discussed quite a few acts of jihad committed by him or others.

Saddiq finally got around to our purpose for the visit. He asked for the detonators. He also asked for hand grenades.

"Don't talk out loud like that," Dr. Rashid told him. Once again, I saw the paranoia and the care these people took to not be over-heard.

So Saddiq rephrased: "Ok; we need 'balls.'"

"No problem. I'll get them for you. What else?"

"Well, we need some weapons in case we are stopped by the FBI when we go to place the bombs. We'll need to defend ourselves and our bombs until they can go off."

Rashid promised to deliver. We finally finished that meeting and returned to Jamaica Queens safe house/bomb factory.

Because the recorder was a little distance from Hampton-El, and because he spoke with an African-American accent, most of the transcribers couldn't understand it. But when they brought in an African-American agent to transcribe, they got a lot of juice from that tape.

Car Thief

Emad S. with Wahid Matrawy (the car thief)

The next player in this opera that I would meet was Wahid Matrawy. He was a very talented Egyptian at stealing cars. Saddiq met with him to place our "order" of five stolen cars. We would not rent a van or car for this operation; jihadists in New York had learned the hard way that rentals are easily traced like what happened in the 1993 WTC bombing. Stolen is a better option. And so again, one jihadist with a needed talent helped another who had his own jihad plan.

We didn't go meet Wahid. He came to the safe house in Queens. Lucky for us he did: we have him on surveillance video discussing the four cars and one limo he would arrange for us.

One vehicle had to be a limo. We were getting the diplomatic plates from the Sudanese there, and we would roll the limo and its volatile cargo into the basement-parking garage of the UN building with no fear of search because of the diplomatic tags.

More Interference from the Suits

We now had the basic bomb materials, and Dr. Rashid and Wahid Matrawy were working on their respective ends. Saddiq wanted to be ready when Wahid delivers.

"What else will you need? How about timers?"

"I'm going to work on them now," I stalled.

Through John and Louie, I was able to get a timer from the FBI.

You can see the video on my website of Saddiq and I working on the timer to get the settings correct. You can hear us counting, "One, two, three, four…"

At that point, Saddiq says, "No I need more time on this, enough time for the brother who sets it off to get back out of the tunnel before it goes off." And so we worked on it some more.

After Saddiq was satisfied that the timer would work, the FBI wanted it back again, to keep it from falling into the wrong hands.

However, the terrorist group knew it was there. If it went missing, someone would notice, and I would be exposed for sure.

I ended up being very angry about the inability of the Suits in the offices to understand the danger I was in on the street and in this cell. How could they not see the simple truth that if the timer I brought went missing, I was in the cross hairs? Sometimes I wondered if that was right where someone wanted me to be. If I disappeared, no one would be around outside the agency to reveal what really happened.

Despite my objections, an agent, I guess, snuck into the safe house and took away the timer. Fortunately, I was the only one who noticed its absence the next day when we worked there. I was furious. Finally, finally, I convinced the Suits, sitting safely behind their desks, that my life was on the line here! Somebody went in again and replaced the timer.

It was ok for it to be there anyway; no bomb was going to be built. The whole place was under surveillance, rigged and bugged by the Feds before we ever started building.

That surveillance in itself is rather funny, because Saddiq, in his paranoia, had me sweep the safe house for bugs about every-other-day. I always did the same trick I had done with the Sheik and convinced Saddiq every time it was still clean and safe, despite the cameras and microphones covering the whole place.

CHAPTER TWENTY
Closing Time

Saddiq had other men come into the project in those last days (the people underground) Tarik Elhassan, Fares Khallafalla, Victor Alvarez (a Puerto Rican we was also called "Mohamed the Spanish") and Amir Abdelgani and his cousin Mohamed all got assignments from the leader of the cell (Saddiq).

As Saddiq became more anxious to get the show started, he recruited those who had the talents and connections he needed. Now everything was happening quickly. Victor Alvarez's assignment was to bring weapons, and he did bring the gun and gave it to Saddiq. At midnight in Saddiq's apartment in New Jersey I was informed that we have a weapon, Saddiq showed it to me and I immediately jumped to document it, I asked Saddiq to make me a cup of tea I put the gun on the floor and I started to lure Saddiq's cat to come close to the gun so when I take the picture I can prove that it was taken in Saddiq's apartment.

The gun with Saddiq's cat

Many more terrorists had entered the cell and they were captured on audio and videotapes via the FBI surveillance equipment in the bomb factory. The case was building, but so was the danger.

Once we had all the materials, the whole situation did get more dangerous just by its very nature. The city was crowded. Volatile chemicals sat in a very hot safe house in a residential district of Queens. Weapons were coming into play.

Saddiq and I made another survey trip of the targets, including the tunnels. I took pictures of the places. You can see them on my website.

We were getting close.

Without telling me they were about to do so, the FBI decided to close the case and pull in the fish before they got away or caused any more trouble – fatal trouble.

PART III

Reaping the Bounty, Paying the Price

CHAPTER TWENTY-ONE
Day of Terror Bust

The day the FBI decided to shut down the operation and make the arrests came as a surprise to all of us. In the early hours of June 24, 1993, the Feds descended on the safe house I had rented in Queens, during the cooking of the witch's brew.

I had been given no indication the operation was being closed and the net pulled tight. The prosecutor who was in charge at that time promised me the opportunity to get my sister's family to safety and my own family as well.

I was in the bomb factory along with some of the others and we heard someone entering the safe house where we were working, mixing, setting timers, etc. And suddenly they were upon us, a SWAT team, dressed all in black and very well armed.

We were shoved to the ground, guns in our faces, and handcuffed with plastic cuffs. As I lay there on the ground, my face in the concrete, a gun to my head and a combat boot on my neck, all I could think was that I had been right all along. This was not going to be a fake arrest. They were going to make me out to be a terrorist, a defendant in the case I myself had built. No, no, no…This was all wrong. James Fox's comments to reporters that the undercover informant hadn't given the FBI any useful information came rushing to the front of my mind.

And then my chest started to squeeze. I couldn't breathe. I knew I was having a heart attack.

The SWAT team did not know my identity before the bust, though they did know there was someone inside the cell, undercover. They didn't treat me any differently than the other defendants. I suppose that was best for my family, because the other bomb builders or members of the cell not yet arrested wouldn't know right away I was the informant.

It took a few hours for the others not present at the safe house that night to be arrested as well. In the end there were ten arrests and, later, convictions based on this case I had been pivotal in building. Fortunately, the cell did not put two and two together and get "Emad" before my family in the US was whisked away to safety.

John Anticev and Louie Napoli took me in their car to Mount-Sinai Hospital. This kept me away from the others in transportation and booking.

The heart attack was, in fact, an anxiety attack – a very well deserved anxiety attack! I thought for sure the FBI really was going to get rid of me to cover up their screw-ups. But here were my handlers, sitting at the hospital all night with me, making sure I was ok.

Good-Bye Salem Family

Once the doctor gave me an injection to help the anxiety pass, John and Louie took me home to the apartment in Bretton Hall. I had called Karin from the hospital about 6:00a.m. "Honey, the Feds took the case down. They're bringing me home in a little while, and we'll have to move out of the apartment."

The SWAT team joined us at the hospital to serve as a protective escort and to later secure the apartment building and our safe removal. When we went into the apartment building, about 7:00 a.m., SWAT team members stationed themselves in every corner. Joining them were FBI agents and U.S. Marshals.

At the apartment, we were met by U.S. Marshal Deputy Alfie McNeil. He was in charge of Witness Protection for my case. He explained again what we already knew – I would go to an undisclosed location, get a new name, have a new life. No contact with the old life at all. Karin was given a choice: stay in our home with her life and her business, or give it all up to come with me. If she came, she would give up her jewelry business, her home, even her name. She could contact no one from her current life. She chose to stick with me. I am glad.

Alfie told us we'd have a few hours to pack a small suitcase for each of us, including Noha and Sherif. Our furniture and belongings would follow us later, after we were settled.

My kids were about ten and fourteen at that time. You can imagine how they felt being awoken at seven in the morning to a houseful of strangers and SWAT team members with guns. That day they would leave their home and their friends. Their lives would never be the same again. Just a few years earlier I had brought them to this foreign country, and now I was tearing up what roots they had managed to put down. I was very aware of the price we were all paying for America.

My son says it was very scary. That was, unfortunately, only the first scary situation I would put him in. Their lives would never be truly normal again until today.

Who Doesn't Trust Whom?

Alfie brought in explosive sniffing dogs to check out the apartment. The dogs went over the whole place, and the handlers indicated all was clear.

"Um," I said, "not exactly. I have five M80's in my drawer in the bedroom. They're from the experimental bomb I did for them, out in Connecticut." I showed them the M80's, and the team removed them. Alfie, however, was very angry that the dog handlers had missed that very obvious explosive.

He wasn't the only one angry that day.

Carson Strikes Again

About this time, a couple of agents sent by Carson Dunbar came in to "sweep" my home for bugs and tracking devices, so the terrorists "can't track your location when your furniture is taken to you."

I was being very cooperative. I had nothing to hide from them. I said, "Sure. Where do you want to start?" They said the bedroom so I took them to it.

When I started to go into the room with them, though, they said, "Oh no, you'll have to wait in the other room."

"Really? Why?"

"Oh, the equipment will be inaccurate if you're in the room."

Red lights and sirens went off in my head! Something bad was about to happen here, I was certain. These guys forgot that I have many hours experience sweeping for bugs and recording devices. They made a mistake right there.

"Oh. Ok," I said. I stepped back out and gave them time to get caught with their pants down. After about ten minutes I burst in upon them. They had removed personal items and documents from boxes under the bed and from some drawers and were sorting through them. One of them had in his hand my retired military ID from Egypt. Being in Arabic, he couldn't read it, but it had my picture on it. I was in uniform. He mistook it for a current military ID and thought he had a big find. He assumed I was some sort of intelligence officer or double agent.

"What do you think you're doing!?" I yelled at them. Full and total surprise.

"Uh…looking for bugs…"

I grabbed the ID from him. He resisted but I prevailed, partly because of my aggression and anger. Yelling, I accused them of doing an illegal search. "You came here to search my apartment with no warrant. This is an unlawful search. I did not give you permission to go through my personal papers. You have no probable cause, and I am not a suspect of anything!

"Get out of my house!" I yelled. "I could sue you and your bosses for this search without a warrant. You are trying to use my ID to make me look like a spy, aren't you? You are not taking it!

"You aren't fooling me! You forget I know about sweeping and recording devices. You made a big mistake! Go tell your boss you aren't smart enough to carry out his plan! Get out of my apartment! Go!"

Officially, I knew I wasn't accused of anything. Unofficially, in the eyes of those who had tried to make me out a spy earlier, I felt I was a suspect. Or rather, I was to be a scapegoat, set up to be a suspect so that I could be shut away, never to tell what I knew about the many flaws behind the desks of the Federal agents.

Of course, if I were discredited and not available to testify and validate the recordings and evidence I had gathered, what would become of the Blind Sheik and those closest to him? The CIA's man would once again escape to continue his reign of terror in America. Did someone want that to happen? But I only thought of that later.

They had once again assumed that because I was foreign, I was stupid. They tried to play games with me yet again. I was so angry and frustrated.

They left without taking anything of mine. After I calmed down, I did hand the ID to Alfie to give to Andrew McCarthy, because I didn't want them to think I was hiding something. But I did not like the trick Carson Dunbar tried to pull on me. It was his mistake and his pride, I believe, that disrupted the first investigation and allowed the first WTC bombing. He wanted to make me look unreliable so he had an excuse for not trusting me and for firing me in the middle of an important operation that led to the deaths of six Americans and the injury of many more, when he had the power to stop it, without even having a plan B it was pure stubbornness on his part.

It was evening when we finally were escorted out of our apartment under the protection of the New York SWAT team and some deputies from the US Marshals who were in constant contact with the chopper flying above for a bird eye vision for security and into pre-arranged safe house and that was the end of my family's normal life and my own life as Emad Salem. We never came back.

CHAPTER TWENTY-TWO
Hats Off to the U.S. Marshalls

In the US Marshall Service, I couldn't tell the Humps from the Suits. They all dressed alike and worked alike and looked out for each other – and for us.

I was amazed by the way they communicated with each other, securing the 12- story building without panic and without a glitch. A helicopter conducting surveillance communicated with the Irish, grey-haired Deputy Alfie McNeil. Alfie treated his Deputies as if they were his own children, with discipline, respect and a great deal of harmonious communication.

These Deputies knew what they were doing, which impressed me greatly. They moved us out of the building without the media frenzy out front even noticing.

At this time, the F.B.I. completely handed us over to the Marshalls and no longer had direct communication with me. Anybody who wanted to get in touch with me had to go through the Marshall Service after that. Each of the several times we were moved over the first few days – and in later moves, as well, I watched a symphony of communication between all the Marshals, played smoothly, swiftly and with accuracy, from car to car, from car to van, from van to private jet.

It all happened with the utmost secrecy and professionalism. I can honestly say, the U.S. Marshall Service is the most efficient federal agency I ever experienced.

I have been through a long journey with the Marshals, who changed our names and identities to avoid the constant threats on our lives. I take my hat off to the Witness Protection Program and to all of the Deputies assigned to protect me and my family for the two years I was transcribing hundreds of hours of audio and video recordings, in preparation for the trial.

Emad S. translating

The Marshalls treated me with more respect as a U.S. citizen than anyone else had treated me. I am sad to say, the reality is that, to the FBI management, I am a second-class citizen and disposable. It was apparent in the way they handled me from their air- conditioned offices. They never looked at my eyes when addressing me. They never even trusted their own Humps, who worked with me hand in hand and did face me eye to eye.

CHAPTER TWENTY-THREE
Security

We spent that night in a safe house, away from the media frenzy that started in front of our apartment building in the early hours of June 25, temporary alias names were assigned to us, shortly after our final departure. We moved the next day to another safe house, and were moved again the next day to another safe house where we settled for about three months as more arrests took place, including that of the Blind Sheik (July 3).

SWAT Team

The New York SWAT team provided manpower and more firepower for the Marshalls until they stopped moving us so much. They stayed with us about a week. Our relationship with them was friendly, so when they were finishing their assignment, we had a farewell party to thank them and end our time together. They gave me a SWAT team hat.

The Magnitude of Security

Life established itself into an odd kind of routine. Our quarters were very well guarded. As a result, they were pretty much windowless, not a good situation for young kids in the middle of summer. There was a female agent who used to go to the trouble of getting them safely outside to play as much as she could.

My family stayed in one place for months, but I did not. Unfortunately, I, who had gotten them into this strange existence, was often gone, driving or flying to destinations I didn't even know.

Now that arrests had been made, hours and hours of tapes had to be translated from Arabic. The FBI had to sift through evidence and solidify charges in preparation for the Trial of the Century, as Andrew often calls it. They had to get ready for a trial, a trial where I was a "critical"[5] witness.

The HRT (Hostage Rescue Team) were now in charge of guarding us and keeping us safe. When they took me to meetings, (which was often, as we hurried to translate) a whole team of agents usually drove me around in a convoy of three black jeeps. But one day, a single agent came in a single car to take me to a meeting.

---

5   McCarthy, p.289.

Always alert to safety issues, as I trusted myself more than anyone else, I asked as we left the house, "Where are the rest of the agents and the other jeeps? Aren't they coming?"

"No. Today it's only you and me."

"Why?"

He pointed upward with one finger and simply said, "the Eye in the Sky." at this moment I thought that is the time where I will be killed. Single agent, single jeep, driving through the woods, it was time for me to be eliminated or that is what I thought. I was so suspicious of that agent and I monitored him waiting for the moment when he will pull out his gun to kill me, so I can try to defend myself. Remember that I was thinking with the Middle Eastern Mentality. The agent was so prompt and kind and delivered me to meet with Andrew Mcarthy in a safe place.

I immediately realized the eye in the sky was a satellite. I realized they were trying to deceive someone who might be watching by satellite image. Someone who knew we usually travelled in a motorcade. Just this one vehicle would be out of routine and they would not think I was in it. It would not appear that I was being moved around.

They were hiding me from the bad guys… but also from the CIA.

I realized at that moment the magnitude of the security we were being given. I now understood why there were agents inside our bedrooms with machine guns while we slept at night.

Translating Tapes Before the Trial

I give the Federal Marshals five stars. They are the top Federal agency in the country, professional, prompt and dedicated.

If you are in the Witness Protection Program, and you follow the rules, they will keep you alive. They adjust the program to protect you.

The translating and preparing took place, as I said, in unrevealed destinations all over the country for days at a time. When they took me from place to place, every step of the way was measured and calculated and washed from any information that could blow our security.

The security was excellent. These men knew what they were doing in witness protection. However, in the end, it is God who determines our safety, and I trust him and myself to look after me.

Bringing My Sister

I found out my sister and her home and family were under surveillance by the Sheik's followers immediately after the bust. I was concerned for her safety. I had expected this to happen. The original Assistant U.S. Attorney on my case, had promised to give me time to take care of my family in Egypt before the Bust. Of course, I had also laid down the condition that I was not to be arrested with the others, and we know how that turned out.

AUSA came to question me, to gather information for the trial, right after I found out my family in Egypt had not yet been secured. He had promised me they would be, that I would have a heads-up before the bust to get them to safety. So when he began to question me, I said "I don't want to answer your questions, because I don't trust you."

"What?" he was surprised.

"I don't trust you because you are a liar."

His face turned red with anger. "Why would you call me a liar?" He was shocked.

"You promised me that you would not pull the plug on the case until you informed me, so I could secure my family in Egypt. Now here I am, and my family is up there hiding in the house, locking their doors. I don't want to work with you."

My understanding is that this conversation found its way back to Mary Jo White, the US Attorney at the time. The prosecutor didn't work with me after that. Andrew McCarthy took his place.

Andrew McCarthy is a person I hold higher than anyone else I have ever met. He is an honest, honorable federal prosecutor, respectable and respectful. I learned a lot from this man in so many aspects.[6]

Andy started to be my contact in the U.S. Attorney's office that was preparing the case, a case that has been called "The Trial of the Century." Andy was lead prosecutor for the case.

He got in touch with the U.S. Embassy in Cairo. A guard of U.S. Marines from the Embassy whisked my sister, brother-in-law and nieces into a limo and back to the Embassy. They prepared visas for them and put them on a plane to the U.S.

As soon as they landed, Andrew called me. "Your sister is on American soil." They were met by federal agents and treated very handsomely.

Andy has worked hard to earn my trust, and he has earned my love, bless his heart.

---

6   See the testimonials in Appendix 1 for more on the relationship Andrew McCarthy established with me right from the start

CHAPTER TWENTY-FOUR
Personal tapes

Andrew McCarthy was the lead prosecutor for the case against the Blind Sheik and his followers, and he was preparing his case. We would meet in secure locations to prepare for the trial that was to come, one that was clearly going to be complicated and promised to be long.

Andrew was talking about something; I don't remember the substance of the conversation at that time. But the subject of trust came up. I said that I didn't trust anyone. At that time I was very upset by the way I was being handled.

I said, "I'm glad I have proof that I delivered all that information to them. I even have it on record."

Andy was startled. "What do you mean have it on record?"

"I have recordings of the agents that prove I told them about the bombing beforehand, that the bomb would go off."

Andrew was shocked now. "You taped the agents? You taped FBI agents without them knowing it?"

"Yes!"

"Why?!" This was a whole new ballgame for him.

I said, "Andy, what do you mean 'why?' Jim Fox said on national TV that I didn't give them info. And I walk into the FBI office and see my picture on the wall as a suspect! And now the agents 'have no recollections' under oath that I told them, 'When the bomb goes off, don't come knock on my door.' That means I am a bad guy, ready to be arrested and thrown in jail with the real bad guys, because I knew things, and I didn't deliver it to them. I knew this would happen. So I had to have it on tape to prove it."

Andrew said, "Oh. My. God. Oh my God, Emad, we gotta have these tapes."

"Oh, oh, oh! No way. If something wrong happens to me, or the FBI comes to arrest me or something, these tapes will be released to CNN, and the American people will know that I was a good citizen and the truth, spoken in the agents' own voices." I went on talking about why I wouldn't give them up.

Andrew, of course, was very wise. He didn't get angry. Of course, he was blown away that he was handling a very delicate, sensitive case, and all of a sudden the star witness has another tape of the FBI. The witness taped the FBI!

He said, "We have to get these tapes. There is something called 'discovery.' The rules of discovery obligate me, as US district attorney, to share any evidence with the defense. Now I know about these tapes, I must have them. I promise you, they will be handled through secure chain of custody and I will give you a copy of each one of them.

As usual, I decided to trust Andy. I told him I would go get the tapes.

"Where are they?"

"In New York, in my apartment."

"Emad, it is impossible for you to go to NY. You know your home is being monitored by the bad guys, waiting for you to come back. You know there may be a frenzy in front of your home in NY now, waiting for you to go there. It's impossible."

I thought a moment. "Ok, but the only person I trust is Nancy Floyd." So they brought Nancy to the safe house. I don't know how they brought her there. But we Stepped away from the others and spoke privately. I gave her instructions - do this and that, go here, go there, there's a key in this place... open my apartment. She knew my apartment because she visited Karin and me and my kids there numerous times. I told her to go into this particular spot in my apartment, do this and that, and she'd find a package, wrapped up and hidden there. That would be the package of tapes. "Bring it back. I trust nobody but you. These tapes are my life. Without these tapes I could be thrown in jail, and nobody would know anything about it."

She said, "Don't worry; I'll bring them."

They took Nancy to NY. The minute Nancy opened my apartment; she was surprised to see Jim Roth right behind her. He is the special agent in charge of the legal division of the NY office. Roth just walked behind her, right into my apartment with three other agents.

Once she had the package in hand, Roth said, "OK, give us the tapes."

Nancy said, "No!" and refused to give them the tapes. The argument escalated to the point where he had to physically remove the tapes from her. It was a physical struggle between them. It came to a physical push and pull between Nancy and Jim Roth, until they took the tapes from her.

As if that were not bad enough, they started to roam all over the apartment looking for things. My desk was in the front room, and they opened my desk drawers. They took a bunch of pictures of my wife and various other subjects, none of which had anything to do with this case. They took some other tapes from that drawer as well as the one from my answering machine.

This was a search without a warrant. I gave only Nancy Floyd permission to enter my house and permission only to retrieve the package of tapes for me. I didn't give Jim Roth or his agents permission to enter my home or to search the other two bedrooms my desk included.

Finally, Nancy got back to where I was waiting with Andrew McCarthy. Andy was sitting at a table, and Nancy and I stepped away as before. "They got the tapes," Nancy said.

"What? Who? Who got the tapes?"

"*They* did." She gestured toward the door as Jim Roth and the agents entered with all my tapes in a small box. They had my pictures, too. I stormed over.

Jim Roth tossed the box on the table in front of Andy. "Here are the tapes."

I immediately grabbed the box. "Who gave you permission to take my tapes?!" I was yelling, with good reason to be angry.

Roth thought he was important, an FBI agent, head of legal division. I was standing face to face with him, the box of tapes in my hand. He said, "Leave the box!" He tried to pull the box from my hands, but I wouldn't give it to him, among what Jim Roth had collected from my desk were some private and intimate photos of my wife and I, which made me furious to be violated to that extent that made me more angry these photos had nothing to do with anything related to the case.

"Shut up and sit down!" Jim ordered in his most authoritative voice, as though I were a child or a criminal, as though I were the one who had violated the law here.

"Oh really! Are you trying to scare me?" I yelled back, ignoring his "authority." He pulled his jacket to the side to expose his gun, to show me he was armed. That just provoked me ten thousand times more!

"Oh really? Now you're displaying your gun? You think you can protect your own gun?" I was so very angry.

Andrew has described me as a pain in the ass. Yes, I *was* a pain in the ass, because everybody was screwing me. Everyone was mistreating me.

Jim Roth stood there exposing his gun, pulling his jacket back to show me his gun and his badge on his belt. And that didn't scare me. I knew he violated the law. I knew he violated *me*, and I was tired of this. I wasn't scared of guns. I had guns in my hand all of my life. And I know how to handle guns. If I was able to take two guns from two big guys in the elementary school, Jim and his gun were no big deal for me. I was really sick and tired of being mistreated. (See my website for more on this story and others like it: http://www.emadsalem.org/Home.php.)

Roth was trying to stand his ground. We stood nose to nose, neither of us giving an inch. His agents started to move in behind me. Andrew finally stepped, literally and physically, between us. In his own book, Andrew says though he himself was unarmed, he could see Emad, a black belt in martial arts, and four armed agents facing off. He felt he was about to lose his witness and lose his case.

When Andrew stepped in, I took a step back. Jim took a step back.

I told him, "You just conducted an illegal search without a warrant. And I'm gonna have your ass sued by my lawyer." I had a lawyer of my own, just because I did not trust anybody. "I'm gonna sue your ass for conducting an illegal search and taking my pictures and my tapes without permission."

Andrew tried to calm the situation down. He promised me that these tapes would be handled by him personally through the chain of custody until he could bring me copies of all of it, and so on and so on. I started to calm down

I went back over to Nancy Floyd. "You betrayed me. I never trusted anybody and now you are one of them. And I don't trust you." I understand now that I was harsh on her. She couldn't do anything about it. It was four guys; they just overpowered her in my apartment, and she couldn't do anything about it. I know that now. But when I yelled that at her, it was the first time I ever saw tears in her eyes. I feel bad that I hurt her feelings, but at the time, I felt so betrayed by everyone and so unsafe with them all.

Andy took the tapes, and they moved into the legal chain of custody. They were legally secured and went through the proper chain of custody. Copies were made and distributed to the defense attorneys. I got my copies, which I still have - more than a couple hundred hours of recording. I have to move them with me from location to location and keep them secure.

CHAPTER TWENTY-FIVE
The Trial

The Judge for the trial was the Honorable Michael B. Mukasey. His commentary on the actions of the defendants was as follows:

> *Judge Mukasey said he feared the plot could have produced devastation on "a scale unknown in this country since the Civil War" that would make the 1993 bombing of the World Trade Center, which had left six people dead, "almost insignificant by comparison."*
>
> -The New York Times, September 20, 2007[7]

He spoke these words as he handed down a sentence of life in prison for the Blind Sheik.

---

7   http://www.nytimes.com/2007/09/20/washington/20trial.html?pagewanted=all&_r=2&

Security During the Trial

My family and I continued to have heavy security as we settled into various places to try to live a kind of stable life while I translated tapes. That was fine, while we were in hiding with very few people aware of our location. Even the FBI didn't know our location for much of that time.

But once the trial started and I had to be in the presence of the men I had spied upon, I was quite concerned. I didn't believe Alfie when he said I would be safe.

"Watch me," he said.

And he and his men DID know what they were doing. I couldn't believe how good they were. Three marshals moved along with me in an arrow formation – one ahead to take any incoming bullet, and one on either side to whisk me away to safety, if needed. I usually wore a bulletproof vest, especially during the time period of the trial.

However, in the courtroom, I did not wear the vest. At first, I really doubted that they could keep me safe without a vest. I expressed my doubts. But the first day of the trial, they took me from where I was staying to the courtroom without any eye seeing me. I just popped into the courtroom. I gave them my best salute.

Trial Testimony

During testimony in the trial, I was portrayed as having entrapped the terrorists by suggesting that we bomb these specific targets. In truth, John Anticev and Louie had briefed me well on what I could and could not say. I was very careful to phrase my questions and statements in such a way that they were not entrapment. There are small differences and nuances of wording that make a great deal of difference.

I had been able to record some of these people, like Dr. Rashid, referring to conversations we had in the first investigation when I was not wearing a wire. Some of the distrust in the beginning may have been because the Feds had no way to corroborate what I told them, to find out if I was giving them the truth. While I found this offensive, I too, have worked in security, and you have to make sure of your sources. The tapes were able to reinforce the conversations I had reported earlier.

Intelligence gathering isn't always so cut-and-dried. If you send me in to find something out, don't tell me, "Don't put your hand in his pocket to get a phone number, for God's sake." Bad guys don't just lay out all the private information you want so you can pick it up nice and neat. You want the number, you know it's in the pocket, and you get access to the pocket? Hmmm, you just don't remember where it came from. You do what you have to do.

I did not mind walking close to this line in order to stop these evildoers who I already knew were planning these disasters.

The interviews I had done in early 1993 to gain the Sheik's trust after the WTC bombing came back to haunt me during the trial when I had to testify.

Much of the Feds' case depended on the audio and video evidence I had gathered. If I could be made to seem unreliable – or worse – all that evidence would be tainted, and the case would lose its basis.

Attorney Lynne Stewart

Lynne Stewart, the attorney for the Blind Sheik, had me on the witness stand, trying to discredit my testimony and me. (She is now in prison serving a ten-year term for helping the Sheik pass along messages to his followers, sadly the Obama administration decided to release her for compassionate reasons at the time she had no compassion for the sixty three Swiss tourists who were slaughtered in Luxor, Egypt due to her information transfer from Sheik Omar to his followers via press conferences.) I pray to God that the Obama administration will not have compassionate reasons to release the Blind Sheik who never had any compassionate reasons for the people he gave fatwas to be killed like president Anwar El Sadat, Refaat El Mahgoob the former head of the Egyptian Parliament, Farag Fouda one of the Famous Egyptian journalists, Hassan El Alfy the former Interior Minister, and the attempted murder of Noble Prize winner Naguib Mahfouz, and so many others.

It went about like this:

LS - "You went on a New York TV station and gave an interview?"

ES – "Yes."

LS – "And you said Sheik Omar is a great guy."

ES – "Yes."

LS – "Is that true or untrue?"

ES – "Untrue."

LS – "So you were lying to the millions of people watching the interview?"

ES – "Yes."

LS – "If you could lie to all of these people, why don't we think you're lying now?"

ES – "Because right now I'm talking to this jury, and I'm under oath. But when I was giving that TV interview, I was under COVER."

Trial

I was glad to have the secret recordings. My suspicion had been well founded that those who had tried to throw me under the bus after the first WTC bombing would have no qualms about doing so again to cover their own screw-ups. When they came up to testify about their evidence, one after another, they said they had "no recollection" of things I had told them or events that I had recorded. Over and over again, one after another, the agents I had worked for and who had put me in danger said they had "no recollection."

They would not have to take the blame for deaths and mismanagement of assets.

But I was very glad to be able to prove that what I said was true and to show that I was NOT a defendant in the case, as some tried to make me out to be in order to shut me up and get me thrown into a federal prison where no one would ever even hear my story, let alone believe it.

Sphinx Trade

Sphinx Trade in Jersey City

It is an Arabic convenient store in New Jersey, Jersey City. They serve the Arabic community in so many ways including fake IDs. I was informed about it by Saddiq Ibrahim Ali at the time he instructed me to rent the safe house in Jamaica Queens to use it as a bomb factory, Saddiq told me that he will make me an identification as a Jew to use it in writing the lease for the bomb factory so I can mislead the FBI if they come to investigate the safe house after the bombings and they think that it is been done by the Jews. We drove from Saddiq's house to Jersey City at the Sphinx trade store and greeted the man behind the counter apparently they knew each other very well then they took me to the back room, snapped my picture, and they named me Ihud Arad.

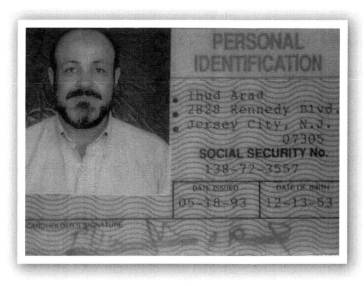

Emad S. as Ihud Arad

They faked my date of birth and my address as well; within twenty minutes I had in my hand a new fake photo identification card. Little does Saddiq know that the FBI immediately had a copy of that ID. The Ironic thing is that this store continued to produce fake identifications until 2001, where one of the nineteen hijackers who drove their planes into the WTC towers also obtained a fake ID from the same Sphinx Trade. I wonder why?

CHAPTER TWENTY-SIX
Trust and Respect

One of the reasons I trust Nancy so implicitly is her respect for me. She knows her job and is not afraid to do it. She follows the rules and is professional. But she has respect for the people she works with, from NYC police detectives to FBI agents to her boss at the Russian Squad, Len Predtechenskis. (Carson Dunbar was the head of the terror squad and was never Nancy's direct boss.)

I was brought up to respect others and to keep my word and be loyal. When you trust me, you put a collar on me called "Responsibility." I must polish and maintain this collar so that it does not rust. No matter what happens, I will guard your trust in me with my life. My integrity, my word, is at stake.

I will never violate Nancy's trust in me, and she never violated my trust in her. I put my life in her hands, and she never let me down. I have extreme respect for this agent.

Special Agent in charge
Carson Dunbar

Later on, when Carson Dunbar or others from his office were trying to discredit me, they attacked Nancy. They tried to dishonor her reputation by implying we had an affair. We did not. Our relationship was completely professional, but it was honorably professional. I did not use her to make myself look better, and she did not do that to me, either.

She was disturbed by the leak to the press that put my life in danger. There were very few places that leak could have come from, and any one of the options was unbelievable and frightening. She was not the only one on the street who felt the agency was failing to police itself.

Someone way up had made some big screw-ups, and yet there was no internal investigation to try to hold that person accountable. Instead, there was every effort made to discredit those who could prove the FBI's shortcomings: Nancy Floyd and me. But for Nancy it was a long and rigorous internal investigation, probing into every corner and accusing of any and every infraction, just to see what would stick. She was accused of the affair with me, but my tapes showed that was untrue. Her finances were scrutinized, but she thankfully kept meticulous accounts, and nothing could be found wrong with her expenditures. The whole thing was ridiculous and went on for many years, when most such investigations end in weeks or months. The whole idea was to discredit her and so discredit me. And again, I wonder what was to be gained by discrediting me? Especially when discrediting me would have invalidated most of the evidence against the Blind Sheik and his terrorist cell. What was someone trying to hide? Who was trying to hide it? Why were there no investigations into a leak about an active operation with someone still undercover for a whole entire month before the case was taken down?

Nancy herself told me,
That is wrong….To have your life put in jeopardy, as
well as such an important case, should have been not
only investigated, but the person who did leak should
have been put under questioning for violating FBI
ethics. The fact that the FBI allowed my reputation to
be smeared along with yours was not only morally and
ethically wrong; it should have been looked into, too.
The FBI presents itself as the agency of high standards.
But when they don't do the right thing as an agency,

they just ignore it – instead of holding themselves responsible for bad choices and bad decisions of management, they are promoted.

I appreciate Andrew McCarthy's comments that after he heard the whole story of my reasonable suspicions, he had more empathy. Empathy is good, and it affirms me on a personal level.

But we have never talked about who was responsible for the way I was treated. Who tried to get me killed – or nearly allowed it to happen.

At least - by leaking my existence to the New York Post and then subtly confirming that I did indeed exist as a mole? We never addressed these major issues that must be addressed to make sure they do not happen again.

The story of my existence, or at least, of an unnamed undercover informant was leaked to the New York Post. Some months after the first WTC bombing, the Post published a story that a second terrorist cell was being investigated. Dov Hiknd, a Councilman for the Jewish district, was being guarded because his life had been threatened. In reporting this, the Post also reported the existence of a second cell. One month later, the same paper announced there was an undercover informant in this second cell.

I found out about the story when my handlers appeared urgently at my apartment door and hustled me off to a safe house. I appreciate their conscientious care of me and their interest in my safety. A dozen special agents thought we should take down the whole operation there and then and just get whomever we could.

But they would not speculate on who leaked this idea to the *Post* to begin with. Their jobs were on the line. They didn't feel they could confront the "leaker" and still have their job secure. The knowledge of our operation lay only with those in the JTTF NY office. The leak had to come from the JTTF in New York. But the agents looked at each other stretched their lips and shrugged their shoulders. (This was just a hint of what would come in the future during testimony about the JTTF's prior knowledge of the plot. The answer, in unison, would be, "I have no recollection.")

In the offices, the Suits, with copies of the *Post* story in their hands, didn't have the conscience or the balls to call for an investigation into who had leaked classified information during an ongoing operation. Leaking information to anyone about an on-going investigation, where agents and assets are in danger, is **never** allowed. But in this instance…*shrug.*

I have to think how convenient it would have been for me to disappear, the victim of terrorists. I could never have told how I was dismissed from an active operation where I was providing valuable information about a looming attack with the potential to be devastating to New York and all of America without even having a plan B. I could never have pointed any fingers and said, "If not for this person or that one, those six people would be alive today." I could not embarrass anyone if I were dead.

I want to state for the American public: in my mind, this leak to the New York Post was a signature on this citizen's death warrant. It was a serious act of attempted murder-by-terrorist to cover up personal mistakes and shut me up.

Fortunately, no matter how high up an agent or a suit is, God is higher. I think God protected me when I put my life and my family's on the line to protect "My America." God was protecting America as well, when he protected me. If I had run away in the face of this Leaker's attempt on my life, Judge Mukasey's words might have come true: "…devastation on a scale unknown in this country since the Civil War."

Judge Michael Mukasey

The Leaker depended on journalists protecting their sources when a Federal agent's reputation was soiled by accusations that Nancy Floyd was "The Temptress who seduced the Spy."

As the Leaker had already tried to kill an informant, I am sure there was no troubled conscience involved in trying to ruin Nancy's reputation in order to discredit my testimony and me.

The FBI is one of the best federal law enforcement agencies in the world. Therefore, I have to ask these questions, and I wait for an answer:

1. Who leaked?

2. Why did they leak?

3. Why was a highly professional and qualified federal agent not defended against such shameful public accusations?

4. Why was there no investigation into the leak?

And last, but most importantly:

5. *Why doesn't anybody but me ask the first four questions?*

I cannot publicly or privately accuse someone without laying out the solid evidence (which undoubtedly exists) that would move my accusation into the realm of legal investigation. I cannot ruin someone's reputation in public without harsh consequences. Why should someone else be allowed to do so?

I cannot voice my opinions about who in the JTTF talked to the NY Post. But someone knows. Someone surely knows. And all who know must face that knowledge within themselves and live with it every day. And they must be afraid the same thing could happen to them that happened to Nancy and to me, because someone got away with it the first time.

On my website, http://www.emadsalem.org/Home.php, I explain why there are no more Emad Salem's to continue ferreting out the evil doers who will do us harm.

A Telling Request

State Trooper Carson Dunbar

One day, after we were in protective custody, my Deputy guard informed me Andrew McCarthy wanted to see me. The guard and I drove to a predetermined spot. A jeep was waiting. Andrew McCarthy got out of the passenger side and greeted me, then indicated I should get in the back seat of the jeep he was in. To my surprise, Carson Dunbar was driving. Between them sat Dunbar's son. I left my Deputy's jeep and got in with Dunbar and McCarthy, sitting behind Andy.

We drove well out into the country before we pulled over. The Dunbar boy, who was perhaps eight to ten years old then, ran off to play among the trees. Carson and I sat under a tree watching him. Andy got out and walked away.

Carson started a conversation that went something like this.

"Emad, I know we had a lot of disagreements. A lot of things happened that were difficult. I just want you to know there is not bad blood, no hard feelings." He paused and kind of teared up. "Now I just want to be able to raise my son." He was asking me not to say or reveal anything that would keep him from being able to do this.

I was a little shocked. "Wait a minute. I hand you a huge case, and in return, you tried to get me killed. You searched my house illegally."

"I was just doing my job."

"You set me up and hung me out to dry in so many ways!"

"It wasn't personal. Sorry if it hurt your feelings. But…I just want to be able to raise my son."

There wasn't any point in saying anything more. He wasn't going to admit his personal motives or that he messed up in any way. He just wasn't going to admit it.

"Sure. OK, fine." I nodded vaguely.

But when we all got back in the car, with me sitting behind Andy again, I took a cassette tape from my pocket. "Carson," I said softly. He looked back at me. I tapped the cassette slowly and deliberately on my hand. "Don't ever try to hurt me again."

"No, No, we're good. No hurting, no nothing." When he saw the tape and heard the tapping, he got the message: "You might think you can hurt me again, but don't try it."

From the look on his face, he understood, and I knew I would have no more need to fear Carson Dunbar or his manipulations. I would be free to finish raising my own children, at least as far as Dunbar was concerned.

Emad S. at the Dunbar Tree

The day after the incident with Dunbar, I asked my security details if we could go for a drive and get some fresh air. I asked them if we could go to the same spot where Carson and I sat under the tree. The Deputy snapped this picture of me upon my request, without knowing why. I just wanted to document the spot where that odd encounter happened.

Unsettled

Many aspects of my time undercover, and the years translating,

and the months of trial were never really settled. Like so many things in human relations, they just kind of came to an end without any explanations.

A senior agent in the FBI, Dan Coleman, taught counter-terrorism at the FBI academy. He was a close friend and confidante of Carson Dunbar, but he liked me. After the case was over, he requested I give sessions at the Academy to try to help agents understand the Middle Eastern terrorist mindset, culture, and motivations. He wanted the agents to see somebody who had not just talked the talk but had also walked the walk, somebody who had been out there in the streets with the agents and the bad guys.

One day at the academy, I mentioned wanting to go visit a cousin who lived a couple hours away. He said he'd give me a ride, drive me there.

On the drive, as we chatted, he said, "You know, it's really amazing you're alive."

"Why?"

"Well, there were just so many occasions where you should be dead, but you're still alive."

I pointed my finger heavenward. "Why don't you ask God?'

"Yeah. Yeah you're right."

On this drive I was also able to ask him a question that had been bothering me. "Why are you mad at Nancy Floyd?"

"She forgot who she worked for – the Bureau or you."

He referred to Nancy's comments in her testimony when she called the agents "chicken" because they said they didn't hear me say, "When the bomb goes off, don't knock on my door." It made Dan angry that she would say that about her colleagues.

I answered Dan. "I think she knows who she works for. But she was brave enough to say what really happened."

I like Dan, but his attitude reflects the Feds' attitude that you stick by the bureau, even when it's wrong, and cover up the lies with silence.

Even when it almost gets someone killed.

CONCLUSION

After Mohamed Morsy won the Egyptian election in 2012, he released many prisoners who were in Egyptian prisons for terrorist acts. Just two weeks after their release, seven of these terrorists had lunch in the US White House. I wonder why?

The war on terror will never be won this way. The US must learn what it does not know that it does not know. We still think we can talk and make deals with the leaders of the Muslim Brotherhood.

They will NEVER make a deal and honor it. Never.

The president of Iraq, who participates in peace talks and is praised by many US leaders, will never be loyal to the US on any deal his loyalty is for the Iranian mullahs since they are both Shias.

The Blind Sheik, after gaining US support, financial and material, for the war against the Russians in Afghanistan, was not grateful to the US. He gained a US entry visa when he was on a watch list, compliments of the CIA, as far as I think. And he was not grateful. He quickly ordered strikes against the US military.

I write this book as a book of healing, so Americans can know that good *Muslims* and Middle Easterners are not terrorists and do not approve of terrorism. Islam does not condone or order terror. It goes against the teachings of the prophet.

But I also write as an instructional book, a warning, so Americans can learn the way *terrorists* think. Jihad in its twisted sense does not know negotiation. A jihadist has nothing to gain by negotiating with who he perceives as an infidel. We must remember this and not think that western rules of engagement apply to the war on jihad. Andrew Mc-Carthy said, in his book "That is the danger when you hand the presumption of innocence to your mortal enemy."

APPENDICES

Appendix 1 – Testimonials

Appendix 2 - Resources

APPENDIX 1
Testimonials

Michael Mukasey
Honorable Federal Judge & Former Attorney General

I lasted on the witness stand in the honorable judge Michael Mukasey's court for six weeks. At the day of terror trial he was calm yet sharp and swift. I never heard him raise his voice during my six weeks of testimony. Yet he treated everybody with kindness and respect. I noticed his sharp intelligence and fairness between the government and defense attorneys. He has a calming effect on everybody including myself. His strong presence in the courtroom obligated everybody to behave accordingly. At the end of the trial he delivered the sentences with intelligent explanatory comments.

Andrew McCarthy
Assistant U.S. Attorney

After I refused to work with AUSA because he did not respect my need to secure the safety of my family in Egypt, Andrew McCarthy became my contact for the US Attorney's office that was preparing to prosecute the Trial of the Century.

I respect Andy more than any body.

I will never forget the first time I met him.

"I'm Andrew McCarthy. I'm the Assistant US Attorney. I'm going to be handling the case, and I am here to learn about the case. So I need to learn what happened."

His words showed I was important to this case. He respected my work and my sacrifice. By learning from me what happened, he was saying I knew what was happening more than he did, even though he was, in his way, a "Fed." Immediately I felt the guy was trying to convey nothing but respect.

He never disrespected me; he never lied to me.

I know some agents felt they had to bluff with me .I lost trust and confidence in everybody. I felt I have to maneuver around the conversation to come to the bottom line, to get to the truth, and to find the reality. Andy did not do that to me. He didn't lie to me to make me do what he wanted. If he promised it, he carried it out. When he couldn't, in some instances, he felt really bad about it and admitted his inability to follow through.

Federal Prosecutor Andrew McCarthy is one of the most honest and honorable men I ever met in my life. He was a great teacher for me, and without his genius brain, we would not have won the case. He mastered the team of prosecutors, who assisted him in the Blind Sheik's trial, patiently and with great success.

Nancy Floyd
New York Russian Squad

She is fast, faster and fastest. Faster in reading, yet faster in writing, and fastest to get back to anybody who even tried to insult her verbally.

That is Special Agent Nancy Floyd.

I saw her in the field, how she carried herself in the world of law enforcement. She did not take crap from anybody. As I said, she was the fastest. Despite of the fact that I was an outsider to the group of agents, they sometimes could not hold their mouths and called her the "B" word. They could not take her straight-up talk, especially with her distinguished Texas accent.

Men do not accept women's superiority in a male-dominated world. Nancy was definitely able to create a "James Bond" image in female form. She was as professional as could be, yet she cared about her source. She remembered my wife's name and my children's. She always started her debriefing with "How are Noha and Sherif?" and she never forgot Karin. She made me feel that she cared about me and my family's well-being. Though she was meeting me to get the information I gathered overnight, she was able to create a caring feeling and made me feel that I was a human being - not a Middle Eastern, naturalized, third class citizen like some of the "Suits" made me feel when I dealt with them.

John Anticev, FBI

You couldn't miss him, even if you tried - more than six feet tall, towering over everybody else. As soon as he opens his mouth however, you are surprised by his soft-spoken tones.

He can be as gentle as his voice suggests. But bad guys who assume he is soft soon find out he is as lethal as could be.

He is Special Agent John Anticev.

John knows how to extract the information he wants, with his soft, gentle voice and sharp, calculating brain he can deliver the honey to attract more bees. He was my case agent. I am fairly sure I am the reason he lost some of his hair, because he had to handle me; and that is not an easy task.

Louie Napoli
NYPD (The Counter Terrorist Squad)

Sharp like a razor, quick and knowledgeable in counter-terrorism cases in and around The Big Apple, he was the "go-to" man in the Joint Terrorist Task Force in New York.

He is Detective Louie Napoli of the NYPD. I always tried to keep him on my side. He is a spicy Italian straight shooter. He lived for his work, and his knowledge was vital during our war against the evildoers.

From an email by Louie Napoli, dated Dec. 2, 2013:

In 1991, *Anticev and I were elated when Emad Salem agreed to work with us; first, because he was an Egyptian Muslim, who spoke the language; and second, he had knowledge of Sheik Rahman and the Islamic Group from his service in the Egyptian army.*

Emad was instructed to join in with members of the Egyptian community who were attending the Nosair trial in New York City. During this time Emad worked endless hours, sometimes as many as eighteen hours a day. His hard work helped him build friendships with individuals close to Nosair and Sheik Rahman. These long hours took time away from his family life (a wife and two small children.)

As Emad gained more acceptance into Rahman's circle, he became one of Rahman's body guard, translators and traveled around with Rahman to other radical organizations, gathering information on individuals not known to the FBI. Emad was able to identify individuals who wanted to avenge Nosair's conviction by killing the Judge who convicted

Nosair and prominent Jewish leaders who attended the trial.

In 1993, after the World Trade Center bombing, Emad was able to locate for us Mahmoud Abu Halima [Abouhalima], one of the participants, who was hiding in his mother's house in Egypt.

Also, during this time, Emad was approached by another of Rahman's translators, Saddiq Ali, who had visions of conducting several bombings (FBI Building, Lincoln and Holland Tunnels and New York Bridges.)

His endless hours with Saddiq led to the arrest of several individuals, including Sheikh Rahman, who Emad captured on tape, giving his blessing for the bombings.

My partner, John Anticev, and I had mentioned on several occasions during our talks to different community groups and in-service seminars that Emad is a true American Hero, for without his endless hard work and dedication, who knows how many thousands of people would have lost their lives and what economic damage to the United States would have resulted.

- Detective Louis Napoli, Retired

Special agent Gamal Abdel Hafiz

He is a smart, articulate, and honest Egyptian born man. He earned a bachelor's degree from Al Azhar University, the largest Islamic University in the world. Yet he is far from being fanatic or radical, he helped me tremendously during the two years preparation for the day of terror trial translating hundreds of hours of audio and videotapes I recorded during my undercover work. I consider him a vital asset for the FBI especially at the time of war on terrorism, and I hope that the FBI can use his endless experience about the Middle Eastern culture and the Islamist's mentality.

APPENDIX 2
Resources and More Information

http://www.alternet.org/blind-sheikh-flashpoint-terror-20-years-after-world-trade-center-bombing

http://pubrecord.org/nation/10726/blind-sheikh-flash-point-terror-years/

http://www.ustream.tv/recorded/29135784

http://www.nytimes.com/1993/10/28/nyregion/tapes-de-pict-proposal-to-thwart-bomb-used-in-trade-center-blast.html?pagewanted=all&src=pm

http://www.nytimes.com/1993/10/31/nyregion/bomb-in-former-s-tapes-give-rare-glimpse-of-fbi-dealings.html?pag-ewanted=all&src=pm

http://www.scribd.com/doc/35383480/The-Man-Who-Risked-His-Life-for-America